How To Start,
Run, and Stay in Business

THE WILEY SMALL BUSINESS SERIES

For the small business owner, success or failure often depends on the day-to-day management of hundreds of business problems and details. Drawing on the knowledge and experience of experts, these concise, detailed handbooks offer you sound advice and vital practical help on every aspect of managing a small business—sales, financing, accounting, advertising, security, and taxes —everything you need to operate a successful business.

OTHER TITLES IN THE SERIES

PEOPLE MANAGEMENT FOR SMALL BUSINESS, Siegel

HOW TO ADVERTISE AND PROMOTE YOUR SMALL BUSINESS, Siegel

SUCCESSFUL SELLING SKILLS FOR SMALL BUSINESS, Brownstone

FINANCING YOUR BUSINESS, Loffel

EFFICIENT ACCOUNTING AND RECORD-KEEPING, Doyle

FRANCHISING, Siegel

PROTECTING YOUR BUSINESS, Loffel

HOW TO RUN A SUCCESSFUL RESTAURANT, Siegel

HOW TO RUN A SUCCESSFUL FLORIST & PLANT STORE, Cavin

HOW TO RUN A SUCCESSFUL SPECIALTY FOOD STORE, Brownstone

FROM RAGS TO RICHES: SUCCESS IN APPAREL RETAILING, Segal

Look for them in your favorite bookstore.

How To Start,
Run, and Stay in Business

Gregory F. Kishel and Patricia Gunter Kishel

JOHN WILEY & SONS

New York • Chichester • Brisbane • Toronto • Singapore

Library of Congress Cataloging in Publication Data:

Kishel, Gregory F.,
   How to start, run, and stay in business.

   (Small business series, ISSN 0272-7811)
   Includes index.
   1. New Business enterprises—Management. 2. Small business—Manage-
ment. I. Kishel, Patricia Gunter. II. Title. III. Series: Small business series.
HD62.7.K58   658′.041   81-3389
ISBN 0-471-08274-0   AACR2

Printed in the United States of America

20 19 18 17

Preface

Starting and operating your own business is one of the most exciting and potentially rewarding activities in which you can participate. In terms of standard of living as well as level of personal satisfaction, there's no limit to what can be achieved through private enterprise. To increase the probability of your success, this book provides the practical information every business owner needs—and presents it in a way that's easy to understand and ready to be utilized.

Many features make this book equally suited for both prospective and present business owners.

Handbook Format. Each stage of business operations—from selecting the right kind of business to financing, insuring, and promoting it—is covered on a chapter-by-chapter basis.

Checklists. These are included throughout the book so that you can measure your progress and monitor any areas of your business that need improvement.

Visual examples. Whether it's an accounting form, job application or inventory card, you can *see* what it looks like.
Approach. The real-world approach to operating a business gives you the information you want when you need it.

Here are a few of the questions dealt with in the following chapters.

- How can I raise enough money to get started?
- What's the right kind of business for me?
- Which is better—a sole proprietorship, partnership or corporation?
- How much insurance should I have?
- What's the best way to find good workers?
- How much should I charge?
- Can I afford to advertise right away?
- Do I need a complicated bookkeeping system?
- What's involved in purchasing a franchise?
- What if I get stuck and need outside help?

Whether you're thinking about starting your own business, or already run one, you'll find the answers you've been looking for in these pages.

Contents

One

Getting Started

In any successful business operation the secret ingredient is planning. The adage that failing to plan means planning to fail is especially true of running a business. Without good plans, a business is totally at the mercy of fate, ruled by laws based on random probability, rather than sound judgment. In this situation, instead of you running your business, it runs you. The way to avoid this is by taking the time to formulate your objectives *before* starting your business. This entails analyzing your reasons for wanting to go into business in the first place, rating your abilities in different areas, and determining which kind of business best suits you.

What's In it for Me?

"What's in it for me?" is the first question you should ask yourself. Forming and operating your own business requires investments of money, time, and energy. In exchange for the opportunity of owning your own business, you give up the benefits that employees take for granted: job tenure, a regular paycheck, paid holidays, vacations, and sick leave, a company insurance plan; and the ability to leave your job behind at the end of the day. It's only logical that you should want to know what to expect in the form of a return on your investment—not just in dollars, but in satisfaction.

The advantages of owning a business. The number of new businesses started in the United States each year is currently growing at a faster rate than the population—clear evidence that owning a business is perceived as offering certain advantages. Those mentioned most often include:

- CONTROL. The authority to make decisions rests with you. As the boss you have the power to direct all the activities of your business.
- CREATIVE FREEDOM. Without the restriction imposed by set policies and the need to go through channels, ideas and talent can be freely expressed.
- PROFITS. The more successful your business is, the more money you can make. Whereas employees' salaries are generally dependent on budget approvals and cost of living increases, yours is directly linked to performance.
- JOB SECURITY. Since it's your business, you can't be fired, laid off, or forced to retire.
- PRIDE. There's the satisfaction that comes from knowing you have built your business into a successful operation through your own efforts.

The disadvantages of owning a business. Being the boss isn't without its disadvantages. Among those most frequently mentioned are these:

- RISK OF INVESTMENT. If the business fails you could lose your entire investment. In addition to this, your personal assets may be jeopardized.
- LONG HOURS. Keeping your business going is rarely just a 9:00 to 5:00 proposition, especially in the beginning. Be prepared to put in 12-hour days to make it work.
- INCOME FLUCTUATION. Instead of receiving a regular paycheck, your income is subject to the ups and downs of the business.

- RESPONSIBILITY. The freedom to make decisions carries the burden of standing by them. If anything goes wrong, ultimately your're the one who's responsible.
- PRESSURE. There's always the pressure to please customers, meet your payroll and satisfy creditors' demands.
- REGULATIONS. You must abide by federal, state, and local laws, as well as the safefy stipulations imposed by your insurance carrier.

Do the advantages of owning a business outweigh the disadvantages? That's something only you can determine. Just as some individuals can be happy only when working for themselves, others prefer to work for an employer. In planning your own business, it's important that you keep sight of your own needs and wants. Will owning a business enable you to satisfy them? And at a price you're willing to pay?

How Suited Am I?

Do you have what it takes to own and operate your own business? It isn't a matter of how smart you are; it's more a matter of personality and behavior. Researchers have found that individuals who possess certain characteristics are more likely to succeed as business owners than those who lack these characteristics. Although there's no total agreement as to the characteristics that are the most important, those frequently cited include—

- MOTIVATION. This is the drive (mentally and physically) to succeed, to accomplish the tasks of your own choosing, on your own terms.
- CONFIDENCE. This is the firm belief in your own capabilities and your chances of success.
- WILLINGESS TO TAKE RISKS. This is the readiness to sacrifice your own security, if need be, in order to accomplish your goals.
- ABILTY TO MAKE DECISIONS. This is the talent to analyze complex situations and draw the conclusions that will make your business succeed.

- HUMAN RELATIONS SKILLS. This is the ability to get along with others, to inspire cooperation, confidence, and loyalty.
- COMMUNICATIONS SKILLS. This is the ability to express yourself and to understand others, so that ideas can be shared.
- TECHNICAL ABILITY. This is the expertise to produce the goods and services of your business.

To rate yourself in these areas and get some additional input regarding your suitability for the entrepreneurial role, turn to the Rating Scale for Personal Traits Important to a Business Proprietor and answer the questions as objectively as you can.

RATING SCALE FOR PERSONAL TRAITS IMPORTANT TO A BUSINESS PROPRIETOR

Instructions: After each question place a check mark on the line at the point closest to your answer. The check mark need not be aligned directly with one of the suggested answers because your rating may lie somewhere between two answers. Be honest with yourself.

Are you a self-starter?
1. I do things my own way. Nobody needs to tell me to get going.
2. If someone gets me started, I keep going all right.
3. Easy does it. I don't put myself out unless I have to.

How do you feel about other people?
1. I like people. I can get along with just about anybody.
2. I have plenty of friends. I don't need anyone else.
3. Most people bug me.

Can you lead others?
1. I can get most people to go along without much difficulty.
2. I can get people to do things if I drive them.
3. I let someone else get things moving.

Can you take responsibility?
1. I like to take charge of and see things through.
2. I'll take over if I have to, but I'd rather let someone else be responsible.
3. There's always some eager beaver around wanting to show off. I say let him.

How good an organizer are you?

1. I like to have a plan before I start. I'm usually the one to get things lined up.
2. I do all right unless things get too goofed up. Then I cop out.
3. I just take things as they come.

How good a worker are you?

1. I can keep going as long as necessary. I don't mind working hard.
2. I'll work hard for a while, but when I've had enough, that's it.
3. I can't see that hard work gets you anywhere.

Can you make decisions?

1. I can make my mind up in a hurry if necessary, and my decision is usually o.k.
2. I can if I have plenty of time. If I have to make up my mind fast, I usually regret it.
3. I don't like to be the one who decides things. I'd probably blow it.

Can people trust what you have to say?

1. They sure can. I don't say things I don't mean.
2. I try to be on the level, but sometimes I just say what's easiest.
3. What's the sweat if the other fellow doesn't know the difference?

Can you stick with it?

1. If I make my mind up to do something, I don't let anything stop me.
2. I usually finish what I start.
3. If a job doesn't go right, I turn off. Why beat your brains out?

How good is your health?

1. I never run down.
2. I have enough energy for most things I want to do.
3. I run out of juice sooner than most of my friends seem to.

Source: Small Business Administration, Starting and Managing a Small Business of Your Own, 1973.

Where did most of your checkmarks go? On the top? On the bottom? Ideally, all your marks should be on the top. If they're not, you have one or more weak spots to consider. It's up to you to find ways to bring about improvements in these areas, either by changing your personal habits and attitudes or by staffing your business with people whose strengths can augment yours.

Goal setting. One way to improve your chances for success is to set goals for accomplishing the various tasks associated with forming and operating your own business. For each goal you should indicate your plan of action and specify the target date for its achievement. Then, as each target date arrives, your actual performance can be compared with your intended performance. Whenever a goal is reached a new goal should be set. In this way you can keep both your momentum and your motivation going at a steady pace. For example, your list of goals might go like this:

Month 1

- Read *How to Start, Run, and Stay in Business.*
- Visit the Small Business Administration (SBA) and gather information on starting a business.
- Do research in the public library.

Month 2

- Decide on the type of business to start.
- Collect as much information as possible on the business.
- Attend one of the SBA's Prebusiness Seminars and any other relevant seminars.

Months 3-5

- Prepare a plan of action to obtain funds, locate and furnish business.

Month 6

- Open business.

Year 1

- Have business break even.

Year 2

- Make a 15% profit on sales.

Years 3-5

- Open a second store.

The goals that you set should all be measurable. In other words, if you want to be a recognized leader in your field within three years, indicate the criteria for judging attainment of the goal—membership in specific organizations, write-ups in newspapers and magazines, sales volume, and so on. Unless there is some standard of measurement that can be used to determine what constitutes a recognized leader, there's no way to know if you are one. Always keep in mind, too, that the closer the goals for your business are to your own personal goals, the greater the likelihood that you will achieve them.

Which Kind of Business?

Perhaps you have already selected the kind of business you would like to start. Or you may be considering several alternatives. In either case, how can you tell if you've picked a winner? Will your proposed business be able to support you both materially and emotionally? This depends on such difficult-to-predict factors as the economy, competition, resources, and the political environment—all of them forces beyond your control. But, it also depends on another factor, which you *can* control—yourself. And this factor must be as carefully considered as the others. A business that's right for a friend of yours may not be right for you. Unless you select a type of business, or a field, that genuinely appeals to you, the odds on your winning are so slight that you're better off not leaving the starting gate.

To shift the odds in your favor, the first thing you should do during the business planning stage is think about what you really want to do. Try to come up with ideas for businesses that you would actually enjoy running, not just to make money but to have fun doing it. The more ideas the better. And as you come up with an idea, *write it down*. Once you start digging into your own background, experience, education, and hobbies for inspiration, you may be surprised at how many different businesses appeal to you.

After you've expanded your list to the limit, the next step is to narrow it down, focusing on those business opportunities that most closely match your own qualifications. For instance, if you have a fear of heights and have never jumped out of a plane, a skydiving school is probably a poor choice for you. If, on the other hand, you're a dedicated amateur photographer and enjoy trying out new camera gadgetry and dealing with people, a camera shop may be an excellent choice.

If you're determined to start a specific business, even though you know very little about it, what can you do to minimize your risk? Find out as much as possible about your intended business before attempting to open it. This can be done by getting additional education, taking a job in someone else's business, researching the business in the library, talking to people in the field, and so on. Even though this may make you postpone opening your doors, the delay will be worth it. Once your doors are open, you'll be in a better position to *keep* them open.

As for those uncontrollable factors that also affect your business, the best way to cope with them is to stay tuned in to what's happening in each area. Some new business owners get so caught up in their own affairs that they fail to keep track of events that may have a direct bearing on their operations. You can avoid this by reading newspapers and magazines, listening to what people have to say, and observing the changes in your environment.

Checklist for Going into Business

Now that you have thought about your reasons for going into business, examined your temperament, and considered the opportunities open to you, the checklist should help you to get started. The questions in it relate to both the formation and the actual operation of your own business. Answer each question yes or no. Be as honest with yourself as you can. This will help you find weaknesses that need improvement and topics that you need to research further.

Checklist for Going into Business

Before You Start	**Answer** yes or no

How about you

Are you the kind of person who can get a business started and make it go? ___

Think about why you want to own your own business. Do you want it badly enough to keep working long hours without knowing how much money you'll end up with? ___

Have you ever worked in a business like the one you want to start? ___

Have you ever worked for someone else as a supervisor or manager? ___

Have you had any business training in school? ___

Have you saved any money? ___

About money

Do you know how much money you will need to get your business started? ___

Have you counted up how much money of your own you can put into the business? ___

Do you know how much credit you can get from your suppliers—the people you will buy from? ___

Do you know where you can borrow the rest of the money you need to start your business? ___

Have you figured out what net income per year you can expect to get from the business? Count your salary and your profit on the money you put into the business. ___

Can you live on less than this so that you can use some of it to help your business grow? ___

Have you talked to a banker about your plans? ___

About a partner
If you need a partner with money or know-how that
you don't have, do you know someone who will fit—
someone you can get along with?   _____

Do you know the good and bad points about going it
alone, having a partner, and incorporating your
business?   _____

Have you talked to a lawyer about it?   _____

About customers
Do most businesses in your community seem to be do-
ing well?   _____

Do you know what kind of people will want to buy
what you plan to sell?   _____

Do people of that sort live in the area where you want
to open your business?   _____

Do they need a business like yours?   _____

If not, have you thought about opening a different kind
of business or going to another neighborhood?   _____

Getting Started

Your building
Have you found a good building for your business?   _____

Will you have enough room when your business gets
bigger?   _____

Can you fix the building the way you want it without
spending too much money?   _____

Can people get to it easily from parking spaces, bus
stops, or their homes?   _____

Have you had a lawyer check the lease and zoning?   _____

Equipment and supplies
Do you know just what equipment and supplies you
need and how much they will cost?   _____

Can you save some money by buying secondhand
equipment?   _____

Your merchandise
Have you decided what things you will sell?   _____

Do you know how much or how many of each you will
buy to open your business with? _____
Have you found suppliers who will sell you what you
need at a good price? _____
Have you compared the prices and credit terms of different suppliers? _____

Your records
Have you planned a system of records that will keep
track of your income and expenses, what you owe other
people, and what other people owe you? _____
Have you worked out a way to keep track of your
inventory so that you will always have enough on hand
for your customers but not more than you can sell? _____
Have you figured out how to keep your payroll records
and take care of tax reports and payments? _____
Do you know what financial statements you should
prepare? _____
Do you know how to use these financial statements? _____

Your business and the law
Do you know what licenses and permits you need? _____
Do you know what business laws you have to obey? _____
Do you know a lawyer you can go to for advice and for
help with legal papers? _____

Protecting your business
Have you made plans for protecting your business
against thefts of all kinds—shoplifting, robbery,
burglary, employee stealing? _____
Have you talked with an insurance agent about what
kinds of insurance you need? _____

Buying a business someone else has started
Have you made a list about what you like and don't like
about buying a business someone else has started? _____
Are you sure you know the real reason why the owner
wants to sell the business? _____
Have you compared the cost of buying the business with
the cost of starting a new business? _____

Answer
yes or no
_____

Is the inventory up to date and in good condition?   _____
Is the building in good condition?   _____
Will the owner of the building transfer the lease to you?   _____
Have you talked with other business people in the area
to see what they think of the business?   _____
Have you talked with the company's suppliers?   _____
Have you talked with a lawyer about it?   _____

Making It Go

Advertising
Have you decided how you will advertise (newspapers,
posters, handbills, radio, mail)?
Do you know where to get help with your ads?   _____
Have you watched what other businesses do to get
people to buy?   _____

The prices you charge
Do you know how to figure what you should charge for
each item you sell?   _____
Do you know what other businesses like yours charge?   _____

Buying
Do you have a plan for finding out what your customers
want?   _____
Will your plan for keeping track of your inventory tell
you when it is time to order more and how much to
order?   _____
Do you plan to buy most of your stock from a few
suppliers rather than small quantities from many
suppliers, so that those you buy from will want to help
you succeed?   _____

Selling
Have you decided whether you will have salesclerks or
self-service?   _____
Do you know how to get customers to buy?   _____

Answer
yes or no

Have you thought about why you like to buy from
some salespeople while others turn you off? _____

Your employees
If you need to hire someone to help you, do you know
where to look? _____
Do you know what kind of person you need? _____
Do you know how much to pay? _____
Do you have a plan for training your employees? _____

Credit for your customers
Have you decided whether to let your customers buy on
credit? _____
Do you know the good and bad points about joining a
credit-card plan? _____
Can you tell a deadbeat from a good credit customer? _____

A Few Extra Questions

Have you figured out whether you could make more
money working for someone else? _____
Does your family go along with your plan to start a
business of your own? _____
Do you know where to find out about new ideas and
new products? _____
Do you have a work plan for yourself and your
employees? _____
Have you gone to the nearest Small Business Administration office for help with your plans? _____

[U.S. Small Business Administration publication *Small Marketers
Aid*, no. 71, 1977.]

For every yes answer you gave, think of yourself as one step
closer to turning your business dream into a reality. Each no
answer represents an area to work on—a temporary road-
block, yes, but, a deadend only if you let it be.

Two

Determining the Best Location

The location for your business is too important to be decided casually or solely on the basis of personal preferences. To do so is to invite disaster. Major corporations are well aware of this. When seeking to relocate or expand their facilities, they sometimes spend years weighing the pros and cons of various locations. In your case, spending that much time is probably not feasible, nor even advisable. However, the same scientific approach that works for big business can work for you.

Choosing the Community

When evaluating a particular community ask yourself the following questions: (1) Is there a need for my product or service? (2) How many customers are there? (3) How strong is the competition? (4) Is the community prosperous enough to support my business? (5) What is the community's growth potential? (6) What kinds of people live there (age, income, interests, occupation)? (7) What are the restrictions on my type of business (licenses, zoning, local ordinances)? (8) Will my suppliers have ready access to me? (9) Is the local labor force both adequate and affordable? (10) Do I like the community enough to live and work in it?

1. *Is there a need for my product or service?* A generally approved business strategy is to find a need and fill it. Will your new or pre-existing business be able to fill a need in the community? If not, a change must be made—either in the type of business you're considering or in the community.

2. *How many customers are there?* Is the number of potential customers large enough to justify locating your business in the community? The closer you are to your main market, the easier it will be to serve it.

3. *How strong is the competition?* Having determined that there is a market for your product or service, it's important not to overlook the competition. Do any businesses already have a foothold in the community? How many? What can you offer that will set your business apart from the rest? If yours is to be the first such business in the community, why haven't others already located there? Perhaps there is some drawback you may have overlooked.

4. *Is the community prosperous enough to support my business?* To determine the community's level of prosperity, take a close look at its economic structure. Is it based on manufacturing, retail, services, or a combination of these? Who are the major employers in the town? What kind of work do the employees perform? How much unemployment is there? Could layoffs in one sector result in an economic collapse—if a plant closes down for example?

5. *What is the community's growth potential?* Are people moving into the community or leaving it? Some positive indicators of growth are land development projects, the presence of department stores and other major businesses, well-kept homes and storefronts, active citizens' groups such as chamber of commerce and PTA and adequate public services (health, education, safety, transportation).

6. *What kinds of people live there?* In addition to the size of the community's population, you should be concerned about its makeup. Is the average age 52 or 22? How much does a typical worker earn? What percentage of the community is married? Single? Divorced? What's the average number of children per household? This type of statistical information—called *demographics*—can be obtained from local census tracts and chambers of commerce. For an even more complete profile of the local residents, you might examine their lifestyles as well. What do they like to do in their spare time? Read? Ski? Sew? Garden? Are they politically conservative or liberal? Data of this nature—known as *psychographics*—tell about the inner workings of people, focusing on their activities, interests, and opinions. Such information can be obtained through questionnaires, interviews, and your own observations.

7. *What are the restrictions on my type of business?* Each community has its own unique restrictions, instituted to either promote or discourage different types of businesses. In selecting your location, make sure that you are aware of these restrictions. If not, you could find yourself prohibited from obtaining business licences or expanding your facilities or receiving deliveries or maintaining certain hours of operation. By finding out ahead of time what to expect, you can avoid unpleasant surprises later.

8. *Will my suppliers have ready access to me?* If you are considering settling in a remote, out-of-the-way locale, your privacy may come at a price. Unless your suppliers have ready access to you, you could end up unable to obtain necessary shipments or paying premium shipping costs. This will of course have a bearing on the merchandise you carry and the prices you charge for it.

9. *Is the local labor force both adequate and affordable?* Whether labor is available and affordable depends on your type of business. If you're opening a diner, there's probably not much to worry about. Short-order cooks are fairly well

distributed geographically. But finding the right chef for an exclusive French restaurant could be more of a problem. The more specialized or technical the work tasks, the greater the difficulty in hiring the right people. And this difficulty increases as the number of workers to be employed increases. As for wages, these vary with the community's standard of living. Will budgetary factors necessitate your locating in a community where labor costs are lower?

10. *Do I like the community enough to live and work in it?* Regardless of your answers to the first nine questions, if you can't say yes to this one, keep looking. Relying on personal preferences alone can be disastrous, but ignoring them altogether can be equally so. The location that is best for your business must also be right for you and your family.

Once you've answered these questions, you'll be in a much better position to rate a particular community's attractiveness. And you'll quickly see that what is an ideal location for one business can be totally wrong for another. A seaside resort, for instance, might just be the place to sell bathing suits, but a bad choice for a furniture store.

Selecting the community where you wish to locate is only half the location process. The second and equally important step is to select a site within the community.

Choosing the Site

Regardless of the type of business you are planning to start, be it a retail, wholesale, manufacturing, or service establishment, site selection will play an important role in its development. Evidence of this was found in a study conducted by General Foods in 1963. The company wanted to know why certain grocery stores achieved greater profitablity than others, so it compared seemingly identical stores carrying the same merchandise and utilizing the same operating and promotional procedures. Management effectiveness was also taken into consideration. Surprisingly enough, the stores that stood head and shoulders above the rest weren't always the best managed. Another factor was needed to explain this—the sites of the various stores. Because of errors in site selection, some of the stores, though well managed, could never hope to achieve the success of the stores with the better locations. Such liabilities as competition, declining neighborhoods, and inadequate parking space were just too much to overcome.

The success of Sears Roebuck after World War II can largely be attributed to its recognition of the importance of site selection. Instead of adding stores in the already overcrowded downtown areas of American cities, where other major retailers were focusing their efforts, Sears decided to open its new stores on the outskirts of the cities. This was where it anticipated the postwar families would want to live. To further meet these families' needs, Sears made it a point to provide adequate parking space as well—something its downtown competitors were unable to do.

The Environment

The site for your business could be in the downtown business district, in a shopping center, in a major street, in a side street, or near highway access. Each has its own unique characteristics, which you will want to consider. Then, given your particular business, you can select the environment that will be best suited to its needs.

The downtown business district. The downtown business district is the part of town where finance, business, and industrial concerns generally have their headquarters. Depending on the community in which you've decided to locate, this area can range in size from a few square blocks to many square miles. In this environment a high percentage of your customers will be employees of the neighboring businesses. And, although they may commute great distances by car to reach their jobs, once there they will generally confine any shopping to what's within walking distance. Peak shopping times, not surprisingly, are during lunch and before and after work. In the evenings and on weekends, sales are likely to drop off. The businesses most likely to flourish in a city's downtown areas are restaurants, shoe stores, bars, department stores, gift stores, book stores, clothing shops, and any other enterprises that cater to the working person.

A shopping center. The development of planned shopping centers and malls, which escalated in the 1970s, has significantly changed things for shoppers and businesses alike. Shoppers could now do most of their shopping at one location without having to drive long distances between stores, or repeatedly search for parking places. Retail and service establishments could attract customers into their places of business simply by being in a popular shopping center or mall. Potential customers, who once might have driven by without stopping, now stopped to look and to buy. Shopping centers clearly seemed to be the way to go—but not all centers and not for all businesses. Before you locate in one, take the time to find out what all the terms of occupancy are. What does your rent cover? Are there additional or hidden charges for shared facilities or services such as parking, landscaping, decorations and signs, walkways, public rest areas, special programs, and joint advertising? What restrictions will you need to abide by? Would your business have to be open during specific hours on certain days? How much value would you really be getting for your money? Is the square footage adequate for your needs? Would your assigned space be in a good location in relationship to the surrounding businesses as well as to the flow of customer foot traffic through the shopping center or mall? Would your business be off by itself at the end of a side corridor, where customers would be likely to pass by without even noticing it?

Some other things to be aware of in evaluating a shopping center are the caliber of management operating it; the mix of businesses represented (Are they compatible or competitive? What quality of goods or services do they offer?); the number of magnet stores (department stores), which draw customers to the center; and the vacancy rate.

Locating your business in a shopping center or mall is expensive, and the various costs associated with such a location might be prohibitive for a new business owner. Furthermore, not all businesses derive any real advantage from a shopping center location. Shoe repair shops and cleaners, which provide essential services, probably would do as well, maybe even better, on a major street where their expenses would be less. The businesses that most benefit from a shopping center or mall location are the ones that cater not only to working people but to nonworking adults and to teenagers. Among these are department stores, clothing and shoe stores, record stores, book stores, gift stores, restaurants, snack stands, ice cream parlors, candy stores, and toy stores.

A major street. Major streets have the heaviest flow of automobile traffic. Though perfect for fast food restaurants, shoe repair shops, cleaners, and other stop-and-shop businesses, heavily trafficked streets can have drawbacks. Getting people to stop is one of them. If your business will be dependent on foot traffic or window shoppers, scouting a location will require more than just counting the cars passing by. What is your assessment of the array of businesses located there (antique shops or auto repair shops?), the desirability of the neighborhood, and the availability of parking? Does the street have a character that will make your potential customers feel at ease there?

If you've decided that locating on a major street is the way to go for your business and you've found the right street, the selection process still isn't over. Which *side* of the street is best? According to market experts, the going-home side of the street is better. Because people do their shopping on their way home from work rather than on their way to work, businesses on the going-home side of the street tend to have bigger sales. Further-more, when given a choice of shopping in sun or shade, shoppers generally choose shade. This means that businesses on the shady side of the street also have bigger sales. If the going-home side and the shady side do not coincide, you might compensate for a lack of shade by erecting an awning.

A side street. Side streets are out of the way and less frequently traveled. They may intersect or run parallel to a main street, but for one reason or another the traffic flow is less there. The main advantage of locating on a side street is lower rent. However, you also have lower visibility, which makes it difficult to attract potential customers.

In order for a retail business to succeed on a side street, it must be able to draw customers to it on the basis of its reputation. Sometimes this can be accomplished through word-of-mouth or advertising. The businesses most likely to prosper on a side street are seamstress and tailor shops, nursery schools, industrial suppliers, small manufacturers, and others that aren't dependent on a high traffic flow for sales.

Near Highway Access. The businesses most likely to benefit from locations near highways are those that cater to the driving public by providing food, lodging, and automobile servicing. Amusements and tourist attractions also thrive on the steady flow of automobile traffic. To make the most of this location, your business must be visible from the highway and easily reached by access ramps. Travelers don't as a rule want to stray far from the highway to find you. However, a less visible location can sometimes be improved by means of a large sign that draws attention to your establishment or by means of billboard advertising that includes directions (Take Frontage Road exit 2 blocks west).

Making a Traffic Count

One way to gauge the potential sales volume of the site is to do a traffic count. This involves more than simply counting each car or person passing by. It requires that you *analyze* the flow of passers-by to determine which are *your* customers. For instance, if you're planning to operate a women's health club, you're not interested in counting the number of men who walk or drive by. Furthermore, if this club is to be very expensive, you can also rule out women who obviously would not be able to afford to join it. The accuracy of your traffic count depends on your ability to assess who your potential customers are. So, prior to doing the count, you'll want to spend some time drawing up a profile of your customers to help you recognize them when they pass by.

Having determined whom to count, the next thing to do is decide the *scope* of the count. Will it encompass just the area directly in front of your store, or will it include nearby or cross traffic? Are you going to count people as they enter the area or as they leave it? If you count them at both times, there's a good chance you will be counting some people *twice*. To guard against double counting, it's essential that you set up strategic check points where your count is to be conducted.

The *timing* of your count must also be carefully planned to coincide with a normal or typical period. If you conduct your count during a peak holiday like Christmas or Easter vacation, it will be too high. Counting on Fridays or on the first day of the month could throw your tally out of balance, too, since these are the times when many people receive pay checks and social security checks.

After you've chosen the time for your count, the final step is to divide the day into half-hour intervals. In this way, you can get both a total count of the day's traffic flow and subtotals for the flows at various intervals during the day. These subtotals will tell you when to expect the heaviest sales each day, which should help you plan your hours of operation. For additional information, many business owners find it helpful to do more than one traffic count and compare the data for the various days.

Rating the Site

You should find it easier to determine a site's desirability if you set up a rating system of some kind, against which each site can be judged. The score sheet shown here is one example. Depending on the specific needs of your business, you may wish to modify it.

Site Evaluation Sheet				
Characteristics	Grade			
	Excel-lent	Good	Fair	Poor
1. Centrally located to reach my market				
2. Merchandise/Raw materials availability				
3. Nearby competition				
4. Transportation availability and rates				
5. Parking facilities				
6. Adequacy of utilities (sewer, water, gas, electricity)				
7. Traffic flow				
8. Taxation burden				
9. Quality of police and fire protection				
10. Environmental factors (schools, cultural and community activities)				
11. Quantity of available employees				
12. Prevailing rates of employee pay				
13. Housing availability for workers and management				
14. Local business climate				
15. Conditions of neighboring buildings				
16. Own personal feelings about area				

Three

Your Building

Whether you plan to lease an existing building or constuct a new one, care should be taken to ensure that the building is appropriate for your specific business. The building you finally decide on should be expected to do more than just keep the rain out. It should also promote your business and help it to function properly. Call these elements looks and livability if you will. Does the building have the looks to get a second glance from your potential customers and, better yet, to make them want to come inside? As for livability, how suitable is the building for your various business activities—selling, manufacturing, administration, shipping, receiving, storage? Unless your building gets a passing rating in both looks and livability, you're in for problems—the most common ones being lost sales, operations headaches, and remodeling costs.

Looks

Forget what you've heard about not judging a book by its cover. Right or wrong, this is precisely what people do every time they pass a building. Even those who never come inside and know next to nothing about your business will form opinions about it on the basis of its outside appearance—its looks alone. As such, the exterior of your building should be thought of as a communications medium, capable of transmitting messages about your business. However, if you aren't careful, it's easy to transmit the wrong message. For instance, it would be a mistake for a store selling discount housewares and appliances to be in a building with a polished marble front and brass handles. Potential customers would take one look at the marble and brass and automatically assume that the store had high prices. A brick or stucco exterior, on the other hand, would get a positive reaction, encouraging people to associate the store with economy and practicality.

Retailing

Nowhere do looks exert a greater influence on the success or failure of a business than they do in retailing. Here, not only must your store's exterior accurately identify the nature of your business—an exclusive shop, for example—but it must also be inviting enough to draw people inside. To achieve both ends —identification and invitation—requires planning and attention to detail. For best results, your store's architectural style, building materials, exterior colors, display windows, and signs should all be part of a coordinated effort. Ideally, each element complements the others and serves to reinforce your store's overall image. More than money, what's needed here is imagination and a clear idea of the kind of store you want to be. Once you know that, it's easier to communicate the right message to others.

Manufacturing

Manufacturing establishments have a little more room for error in the looks department than do retailers. This is because they are less dependent on their ability to draw customers inside their places of business. Customers generally don't see the plants of the companies they do business with. Orders are usually placed through wholesalers and sales representatives or by mail. Potential customers who do visit a plant are generally more interested in examining the production facilities than in admiring the building. Although the looks of your building take a back seat to its livability, this isn't to say that looks should be ignored. The exterior of your building makes a statement about the quality of the products you sell, your company's policies, and the level of success it's achieved. A rundown, unattractive building can only reflect badly on your business.

Services

Depending on the service you offer, the importance of looks can vary. Some services are so specialized that their clients actually seek them out and go to some trouble to find them (consultants, automobile repair shops, cooking schools, landscape artists). Others, such as shoe repair shops and cleaners, are frequented so regularly that customers hurry in and out, barely even noticing how the facilities look. These places don't have to use looks to pull customers in because they are coming in already. But not all services find it this easy to attract customers. Restaurants and hotels, for instance, rely a great deal on drop-in customer traffic. The more inviting their buildings, the better it is for business.

Livability

Just because a building is deemed to conform to the local building codes doesn't make it suitable for any and all businesses. The difference between a livable building and one that's impossible depends on what you intend to do with it. The same building that's a dream come true for an automobile repair shop would probably be a nighmare for a jewelry shop. The best way to avoid settling into the wrong building is to consider the building in terms of its construction, space, design, and accessibility.

Is the building's *construction* such that it will be both safe and serviceable for your business? A manufacturer, utilizing heavy equipment, needs a building constructed of materials that can hold up to heavy wear, reduce noise, and resist fire. Cement and steel win out over wood and glass.

Does the building provide too much *space*, or too little? Is there room for expansion later, should the need arise? For optimum operating efficiency, it's important to strike a balance between your present and future needs for space.

Can effective use be made of the building's *design*? This requires that the relationship between the building's selling, work, and storage areas be compatible with your business activities.

Is the building readily *accessible* to both your customers and delivery personnel? Steps, entrances (their number and location), and loading facilities all play an important role in your day-to-day operating efficiency.

Layout

Layout refers to the physical set-up of furniture and fixtures, equipment, merchandise, and supplies within your building. The better your layout, the easier it is for workers to do their jobs and for customers to shop. Conversely, a bad layout can be the cause of inefficiency and lost sales.

Arriving at the right layout involves more than just moving things around and hoping for the best. It involves arranging them in a way calculated to derive the maximum benefit from the space available. The objective is to display merchandise and services to their best advantage, conserve time and motion, and fully utilize equipment. For retail businesses this translates into increased customer traffic and sales. For manufacturing and service businesses this means increased productivity and sales.

Retailing

In retailing, the main function of your layout is to direct the flow of customer traffic throughout your store. This is a two-stage process, first drawing customers into your store and then guiding them from one location to the next within it. Rather than having customers wander haphazardly, or even turn around and walk back outside, an effective layout leads customers where *you* want them to go. En route, exposure to your merchandise increases the number of purchases made. It sounds easy. And it is, if you apply a few tested principles.

1. *Study your customers' shopping habits.* Find out which items customers purchase regularly and which ones only occasionally. Your observations should also help you differentiate between impulse items and demand items. Impulse items are purchased on the spur of the moment, without any planning. Demand items are purchased deliberately, according to plan.

Once you know how your customers shop, you can arrange your merchandise accordingly. Take a grocery store, for instance. Where are the meat, dairy, and produce items usually located? At the back of the store or along the side walls, running from front to back. This gets customers to walk deep into the store, in order to reach them. Since these are demand items, customers don't mind the inconvenience. What's more, because these are regular purchases, customers can be counted on to seek them out repeatedly. This isn't true of such items as candy, potato chips, and magazines. As impulse items, they have to be seen to sell. Unless they are in highly visible locations—next to the checkout counter, for example—their sales will drop.

2. *Create visually appealing merchandise displays.* Unless your displays have eye appeal, customers will ignore them. How important is this? According to a group of independent retailers surveyed by the National Retail Merchants Associa-

tion, one out of every four sales can be attributed to merchandise display. Other stores have credited displays for as much as 50 percent of their sales.

To improve your displays, notice the displays in other stores, read trade magazines, and ask your merchandise suppliers for tips. Many manufacturers will provide retailers with ready-made displays of their product at little or no charge.

3. *Keep merchandise displays fresh.* Even the most dramatic display starts to look commonplace when it's been left up too long. Don't let yours become permanent fixtures.

4. *Coordinate merchandise displays.* Merchandise that goes together should be displayed together. In this way customers are stimulated to purchase more than a single item. A customer purchasing a man's shirt is likely to buy neckties to go with it. Displaying sun glasses, suntan oil, and beach towels together is a good way to increase the sale of all three items.

5. *Create a pleasant shopping environment.* Make your store an enjoyable place in which to shop. In addition to being clean and attractive, it should have appropriate lighting and adequate temperature controls and ventilation. Conveniently located drinking fountains and rest rooms are also a plus.

6. *Utilize space according to its value.* Space directly in the path of customer traffic has the greatest sales potential and therefore the greatest value. The most valuable space of all is directly in the front of the store where customer traffic is the heaviest. The space having the least value is farthest from the traffic flow, generally in the back of the store.

Given these differences in value, it's advisable to differentiate between your selling and nonselling activities and allocate your least valuable space to nonselling activities (administration, shipping and receiving, storage, and customer service). This allows more valuable space to be utilized to generate sales. In so doing, impulse items should be located as close to the traffic flow as possible (preferably at the front of the store), and demand goods can be located farther away, in space having less value.

Manufacturing

In a manufacturing establishment the main function of your layout is to increase productivity. Whereas in retailing a layout directs the flow of customer traffic throughout the store, here it directs the flow of raw materials throughout the production process. An effective layout provides for the most efficient utilization of personnel and equipment with minimum unnecessary movement of materials.

The two most commonly used are the product layout and the process layout. A company that produces a steady flow of standardized products, such as a manufacturer of machine parts, would use a *product layout.* Here equipment is arranged in an assembly line format that corresponds to the sequence of production steps for each product. Raw materials are then located at the points where they are needed and added to the line as the unfinished products pass by. A company (such as a clothing manufacturer) whose products are nonstandardized or produced in varying quantities, according to customer orders, is unable to operate this way. Instead, it would use a *process layout.* Here separate processing departments are maintained and each product passes through only those processing stages it requires. Unlike the product layout, this involves additional movement of unfinished goods and leaves some equipment idle, while other equipment struggles to function beyond capacity. These problems can be partially remedied through efficient scheduling and by keeping a close watch on production activities to streamline them wherever possible.

Services

Service establishments fit into two categories: those oriented toward merchandising (beauty salons, restaurants, hotels) and those oriented toward processing (automobile repair shops, cleaners, plumbers). Layouts for merchandise-oriented businesses normally are similar to those of retail operations, whereas processing services tend to follow manufacturing layouts. The reason for these differences stems from their respective goals: to increase customer traffic or to increase productivity.

Rating Your Building

The Building Evaluation Sheet can help you to get a better idea of a building's ability to meet the specific needs of your business. This can be useful both in selecting the building in which you want to locate and in designing your layout for optimum efficiency.

Building Evaluation Sheet				
Characteristics	Grade			
	Excel-lent	Good	Fair	Poor
1. Physical suitability of building				
2. Type and cost of lease				
3. Overall estimate of quality of site in 10 years				
4. Provision for future expansion				
5. History of building				
6. Exterior of building in promoting your business				
7. A safe environment for customers and employees				
8. Conformity to all zoning requirements				
9. Ready accessibility for customers				
10. Effectiveness of merchandise displays				
11. Pleasantness as place to shop				
12. Quality of lighting				
13. Utilization of space according to its value				
14. Layout in facilitating movement of employees and materials				

Four

Structuring the Business

The type of legal form that you select for your new business can be crucial in determining its success. Your ability to make decisions rapidly, compete in the marketplace, and raise additional capital when needed is directly related to the legal structure of your business.

There are three legal forms to choose from: sole proprietorship, partnership, and corporation. No one form is better than another. Each has its advantages and disadvantages. The important thing is to ascertain the legal form of business that will work best for you.

Some questions you should ask yourself: What do I already know about this type of business? In what areas of the business will I need help? How much money will I need to get started? What sources of money will be available to me later? What kinds of risks will I be exposed to? How can I limit my liability? What kinds of taxes will I be expected to pay?

Sole Proprietorship

More than 75 percent of all businesses in the United States today are sole proprietorships. This means that they are owned by just one person. And, more often than not, that person is directly involved in the day-to-day operation of the business.

As a sole proprietor, you're in the driver's seat. In addition to having total control over your business, you have total responsibility for it. Just as all profits from its operation will be yours, so will all its debts and liabilities be yours as well.

Advantages of a Sole Proprietorship

You're the boss. As a sole proprietor, you have the freedom to run your business in any legal way you choose. You can expand or contract your business; add or drop products or services; and hire, promote, and fire personnel. This ability to make decisions quickly, without having to wait for committee approval, lets you take advantage of timely opportunities. If you are looking for maximum control and minimum government interference, the sole proprietorship could be just the thing.

It's easy to get started. The sole proprietorship is by far the simplest legal form you can choose. There's no legal expense or red tape in getting started. All you need to do is obtain the assets and commence operations. In some instances, local or state licenses may be required, such as if food or beverages are to be sold. But more often it's just a matter of hanging up your shingle.

You keep all profits. All profits from a sole proprietorship go to the owner. You are not obligated to share them with anyone else. It's up to you whether to keep them for your personal use or reinvest them in the business.

Income from the business is taxed as personal income. The government considers income derived from a sole proprietorship to be part of the owner's income. As such, you will have no separate income tax to pay. Furthermore, losses incurred by the business can be deducted from your personal income tax.

You can discontinue your business at will. Should you decide you want to go on to something new, dissolving your business is quite simple. Without the necessity to get second opinions, divide up shares, or process paperwork, you need only cease operations.

Disadvantages of a Sole Proprietorship

You assume unlimited liability. A sole proprietor is responsible for all business debts or legal judgments against the business. In the event that these exceed the assets of the business, your own personal assets — home, automobile, savings account, investments — can be claimed by creditors. In other words, your financial liability is not limited to the amount of your investment in your business, but extends to your total ability to make payment. This unlimited liability is the sole proprietorship's worst feature. (Methods for protecting yourself are discussed in Chapter 12.)

The investment capital you can raise is limited. The amount of investment capital available to your business is limited to the money you have or are able to borrow. Unlike partnerships or corporations, which can draw on the resources of others, you will have to provide the total investment for your business.

You need to be a generalist. Anyone who starts a sole proprietorship must be prepared to perform a variety of functions, ranging from accounting to advertising. Most new sole proprietors can't afford the luxury of hiring specialists for these tasks. Even if you can, you have to understand what they're doing, since you're the one who will be held liable for their actions.

Retaining high-caliber employees is difficult. You may have difficulty in holding on to your best employees because they want more than you are offering them—namely, part ownership in your business. For these employees a good salary and bonuses usually won't be enough. Your only recourse is to let them go or to convert your sole proprietorship to a partnership.

The life of the business is limited. The death of the owner automatically terminates a sole proprietorship, as does any other unforeseen occurrence (long term illness, for example) that keeps the owner from operating the business. Since there is no one else to carry on, the business just ceases to function.

Partnership

A partnership exists when two or more people share in the ownership of a business. By agreement, they determine the amount of time and money each partner will invest in the business and the percentage of the profits that each will receive. The extent of each partner's authority and liability must also be made clear.

In order to avoid misunderstandings later, everything that has been agreed to should be put in writing, preferably with the assistance of an attorney. The importance of a written partnership agreement cannot be overemphasized. In the absence of such a document, the courts can resolve any disputes that arise, but the outcome might not be to your liking.

Here is some of the information which should be included in your partnership agreement:

- Each partner's responsibilities and authority.
- The extent of each partner's liability.
- The amount of capital each partner is investing in the business.
- How profits and losses are to be shared.
- How disputes between the partners are to be resolved.
- Arrrangements for the withdrawal or admission of partners.
- How assets are to be distributed should the business be dissolved.

Advantages of a Partnership

Two heads are better than one. In a partnership you have the advantage of being able to draw on the skills and abilities of each partner. Ideally, the contributions that each partner is able to make to the business complement those of the other partners. For instance, one partner oversees accounting functions, another is in charge of production, another handles sales.

It's easy to get started. Starting a partnership is relatively easy. Although it entails additional cost and more planning than a sole proprietorship (selecting partners, preparing the partnership agreement, and so on), red tape is minimal.

More investment capital is available. Your company's ability to increase capital can be enhanced by simply bringing in more partners. Unlike a sole proprietorship, which can draw on the financial resources of only one individual, in a partnership you have the combined resources of the partners.

Partners pay only personal income tax. Partnerships are taxed the same as a sole proprietorship. The total income of the business is considered to be the personal income of the partners. This means there is no separate business income tax to pay, and business losses are deductible from each partner's income tax.

High-caliber employees can be made partners. Partnerships are able to attract and retain high-caliber employees by offering them the opportunity to become partners. This method of employee motivation has been particularly successful in the legal and accounting professions.

Disadvantages of a Partnership

Partners have unlimited liability. Like sole proprietors, partners are responsible for all debts or legal judgments against the business. This liability is even worse for partners than it is for sole proprietors because, as a partner, you are responsible not only for your own debts but for those of your partners. Should they incur liabilities, you could be left holding the bag. And remember that even though your investment in the business may be minimal, your losses could be substantial. Your liability extends beyond the amount of your investment to include your personal assets as well.

Profits must be shared. All profits resulting from the partnership must be distributed among the partners in accordance with the partnership agreement. What percentage of the profits is to be reinvested in the company must be decided by the partners. Your wishes in this matter represent only one viewpoint.

The partners may disagree. Disputes among partners can literally destroy a partnership. One partner's desire to expand the business can go against another partner's goal of cutting costs. Should your money be spent on improving your product or on promoting it? When key decisions must be made, the feelings of trust and admiration that drew you together as partners can disintegrate. If this is to be avoided, you must give your full attention to selecting partners and drawing up the partnership agreement. Foresight in the planning stage can pay off later.

The life of the business is limited. As with a sole proprietorship, the life of a partnership is limited. Should one of your partners withdraw from the business or die or become too ill to carry on, the partnership is automatically dissolved. Though it is possible for the remaining partners to reorganize the business, the financial interest of the departing partner must first be paid. Furthermore, any time a new partner is admitted to the business, dissolution of the partnership is mandatory. A new partnership, reflecting the addition of the new partner, must be formed.

Limited Partnerships

Because of the unlimited liability that partners are subject to, you may be reluctant to assume the risk. One way around this is to form a limited partnership. In a limited partnership there are two kinds of partners—general and limited. *General partners* assume unlimited liability for the business. The liability of *limited partners* is confined to the amounts of their investments. However, in exchange for this limited liability, limited partners are restricted from taking an active role in the company's management. And the withdrawal of a limited partner from the business does not necessarily dissolve the partnership, should others wish it to continue.

In a limited partnership the risk can be shifted from one partner to another. It cannot be avoided entirely, though, since every limited partnership must have at least one general partner. If you decide to set up a limited partnership, public notice to this effect, stating that one or more partners have limited status, must be made. Otherwise it is assumed that a general partnership exists, in which all partners have liability.

Other Partners

Within the scope of the partnership format, there are four other types of partners you may wish to consider.

Silent partners invest money in a business but take no active role in its management, nor do they share liability. They are primarily interested in getting a return on their investment.

Secret partners are active in the management of the business, but are not known to be partners. Although they want to participate in running the business, they don't want the public to know about their involvement.

Dormant partners are neither active in the business nor known to the public. Like silent partners, they are concerned with getting a return on their investment. Like secret partners, they want to maintain their privacy.

Nominal partners aren't partners at all, but by their behavior they lead the public to believe that they are. An example of this is the person who permits his name to be associated with the business in exchange for a fee.

Depending on your company's needs, one or more of these kinds of partners may be right for you.

Joint Venture

The kinds of partnership just described all share the intention of being ongoing businesses. A joint venture differs from these in that it is a partnership set up for a specific purpose of limited duration. For example, suppose you and a friend decided to buy, renovate, and resell a house together. Your joint venture would start when you purchased the house and end when you sold it. As for your taxes, joint ventures are taxed the same as partnerships.

During the life of such a joint venture, each partner is subject to unlimited liability. So the same caution should be exercised in selecting a joint venture partner as in selecting any other partner. Also, problems can be avoided by consulting an attorney and putting the terms of your joint venture agreement in writing.

Corporation

A corporation differs from other legal forms of business in that the law considers it to be an artificial being, possessing the same rights and responsibilities as a person. Unlike a sole proprietorship or a partnership, a corporation has an existence separate from its owners. As such, it can sue and be sued, own property, agree to contracts, and engage in business transactions. Additionally, since a corporation is a separate entity, it is not dissolved with every change in ownership. The result of this is that corporations have the potential for unlimited life.

The Corporate Charter

In order to form a corporation you must be granted a charter by the state in which your business resides. Each state sets its own requirements and fees for the issuance of charters. The cost for incorporating a small business usually ranges from $500 to $1,500. Generally, your charter must include such information as this:

- Your corporation's name.
- Names of principal stockholders.
- Number and types of shares to be issued.
- Place of business.
- Type of business.

Stockholders

Each person who owns stock in your corporation is a co-owner with you in the business. This does not mean that every stockholder will actively participate in your company's management, or even be associated with it in any way, other than by purchasing shares of the corporation's stock. They are guaranteed the right to vote on the members of the corporation's board of directors and on certain major corporate policies.

Enabling people to become co-owners in a business in this way benefits both the corporation and the stockholders. The corporation is able to obtain investment capital and the stockholders can share in whatever profits the corporation earns. These profits are distributed to stockholders in the form of dividends. Furthermore, since stock is transferable, stockholders are free to sell their stock at any time and receive the current market value for it.

The Board of Directors

The board of directors represents the stockholders and is responsible for protecting their interests. Board members are elected annually, usually for one-year terms, which can be renewed indefinitely by means of the election process. Since the number of votes that stockholders can cast is related to the number of shares they have, major stockholders can virtually elect themselves to the board.

The board of directors generally concerns itself with determining corporate policies, rather than taking care of day-to-day operations. To handle these, the board appoints the chief executive officer and other top corporate officers—vice presidents, secretary, treasurer, and so on. They, in turn, see that the policies stipulated by the board of directors are implemented.

Advantages of a Corporation

Stockholders have limited liability. One of the most attractive advantages of the corporate form of business is that the owners have limited liability. Investors are fiancially liable only up to the amounts of their investments in the corporation. This limited liability ensures that creditors of the corporation cannot touch your personal assets.

Corporations can raise the most investment capital. You can increase the investment capital in your corporation simply by selling more shares of stock. Whereas sole proprietorships and partnerships are limited in the number of owners they can have, a corporation can have any number of owners.

Corporations have unlimited life. Because of its status as a legal entity, a corporation has its own identity. Unlike sole proprietorships and partnerships, whose lifespans are linked to those of their owners, it is possible for your corporation to exist indefinitely. The withdrawal of stockholders, corporate officers, or employees will not terminate its existence.

Ownership is easily transferable. Ownership in a corporation is easily transferable from one person to another. Investors can buy and sell shares of stock as they please without seeking the prior approval of anyone. In addition to providing investors with maximum control over their investments, this enables your corporation to go on operating without disruption.

Corporations utlilize specialists. Because of the separation of ownership and management, the corporate form of business can most effectively utilize the services of specialists. Unlike sole proprietorships and partnerships, which tend to rely on the skills and abilities of the owners to perform each function, corporations employ specialists. The availability of specially trained personnel leads to higher productivity and increased efficiency.

Disadvantages of a Corporation

Corporations are taxed twice. Unlike sole proprietorships and partnerships, corporations and their owners are taxed separately. In what amounts to double taxation both the income your corporation earns and the income you as an individual earn are taxed. This is the primary drawback to the corporate form. However, as your business's income increases, this disadvantage eventually becomes an advantage, because the limit on corporate taxation is lower than that for personal income tax. The highest rate at which a corporation can be taxed is 46 percent as compared to 70 percent for individuals.

Corporations must pay a capital stock tax. In addition to paying a corporate federal income tax, corporations must pay a capital stock tax. This is an annual tax on outstanding shares of stock which is levied by the state in which the business is incorporated.

Starting a corporation is expensive. More expense is involved in starting a corporation than is involved in starting any other legal form of business. There are the costs for legal assistance in drawing up your charter, state incorporation fees, and the purchase of record books and stock certificates. All these require expenditures not only of money but of time.

Corporations are more closely regulated. The government regulates corporations much more closely than it does any other forms of business. Numerous state and federal reports must be filed regularly. And, each year, corporations are required to prepare, print, and distribute an annual report summarizing the company's activities during the preceding year. Often specialists are retained on staff solely for the purpose of providing the data for these reports.

THE ADVANTAGES AND DISADVANTAGES
OF EACH LEGAL FORM OF OWNERSHIP

Sole Proprietorship

Advantages

1. You're the boss
2. It's easy to get started
3. You keep all the profits

4. Income from business is taxed as personal income
5. You can discontinue your business at will

Disadvantages

1. You assume unlimited liability
2. The investment capital you can raise is limited
3. You need to be a generalist
4. Retaining high-caliber employee is difficult
5. The life of the business is limited

Partnership

Advantages

1. Two heads are better than one
2. It's easy to get started
3. More investment capital is available
4. Partners pay only personal income tax
5. High-caliber employees can be made partners

Disadvantages

1. Partners have unlimited liability
2. Profits must be shared
3. The partners may disagree

4. The life of the business is limited

Corporation

Advantages

1. Stockholders have limited liability
2. Corporations can raise the most investment capital
3. Corporations have unlimited life
4. Ownership is easily transferable
5. Corporations utilize specialists

Disadvantages

1. Corporations are taxed twice
2. Corporations must pay capital stock tax
3. Starting a corporation is expensive
4. Corporations are more closely regulated

Subchapter S Corporation

If you are interested in forming a corporation, but hesitate to do so because of the double taxation, there is a way to avoid it. If you form a Subchapter S corporation, your business can be taxed as a partnership. However, in order to qualify as a Subchapter S corporation, your business must meet these requirements:

- It must be a domestic corporation (one created or organized in the United States or under its laws).
- It must not be a member of an affiliated group. (An affiliated group owns stock in another corporation, although the government permits certain exceptions to this).
- It must have only one class of stock; that is, each share of stock must have equal rights and responsibilities.
- It must not have more than 15 shareholders. (Husband and wife are considered to be one person; others are counted separately.)
- It must have only individuals or estates as shareholders. (Partnership or corporate shareholders aren't permitted.)
- It must not have a nonresident alien as a shareholder.

Other requirements, as stipulated by the Internal Revenue Service, are these:

- At least 20 percent of the corporation's gross receipts for a tax year must be from sources inside the United States.
- Not more than 20 percent of the corporation's gross receipts for a tax year can be from royalties, rents, dividends, interest, annuities, and sales or exchange of stock or securities. (These are known as passive investment income.)

Licenses

Depending on your type of business and its location, you may have to obtain one or more licenses. Licenses can be required at the local, state, and federal levels for a variety of reasons:

- To ensure that the practitioners of various services are competent (architects, pharmacists, accountants, cosmetologists, and so on).
- To maintain health and safety standards.
- To achieve compliance with zoning restrictions (for example, a factory would not be licensed to operate in a residential neighborhood).
- To protect the community against fly by night con artists looking for a fast buck.

In addition to regulating business, licenses also serve as a source of income to the branch of the government granting them.

Local licenses. Regulation at the local level is generally concerned with enforcing zoning laws, building codes, and health and safety standards. Hotels, restaurants, nightclubs, and movie theaters all need local business licenses.

State licenses. At the state level licenses may be required for entry into certain professions (marriage counselors, barbers, contractors, insurance adjusters, and so on). These licenses, which are granted on the basis of proven competence, are issued for a limited term and must be renewed at stipulated intervals. Other regulations pertaining to unfair trade practices, zoning, and safety may also be enforced at the state level by means of the licensing process.

Federal licenses. A federal license is usually required if the activities of your business are conducted in more than one state. Among the other businesses that must obtain federal licenses are those that use government property, those that produce medicines, and those that operate radio or television stations.

In order to determine which, if any, licenses are required for your type of business, you should contact the various governmental branches before commencing operations.

Structuring the Business Checklist

To make sure that you have selected a legal form that's appropriate for your business and know the steps to take in adopting it, answer the questions in the Structuring the Business Checklist on page 52.

Structuring the Business Checklist

	Answer yes or no
1. Do you know the advantages and disadvantages of each of the following legal forms?	
Sole Proprietorship	_____
Partnership	_____
Corporation	_____
2. Is it clear to you why any partnership that is formed should have a written partnership agreement?	_____
3. Do you know what information to include in a partnership agreement?	_____
4. Are you aware of the difference between a general and a limited partnership?	_____
5. Can you describe the characteristics of each of the following partners?	
Silent	_____
Secret	_____
Dormant	_____
6. Do you know what a joint venture is?	_____
7. Do you know what steps are required to incorporate your business?	_____
8. Have you considered the benefits to be derived from forming a Subchapter S corporation?	_____
9. Have you found out what licenses, if any, are required for your business?	_____
10. Do you know the costs of obtaining the licenses you need?	_____
11. Have you determined whether the services of an attorney are needed in setting up your business?	_____
12. Will the legal form of business that you have selected be compatible with your particular requirements?	_____

Five

Recordkeeping

Maintaining good financial records is a necessary part of doing business. The increasing number of government regulations alone makes it virtually impossible to avoid keeping detailed records. But just as important as the need to keep records for the government, is the need to keep them for yourself. The success of your business depends on them.

The Value of Good Records

An efficient system of recordkeeping can help you to:

- Make management decisions.
- Compete in the marketplace.
- Monitor performance.
- Keep track of expenses.
- Eliminate unprofitable merchandise.
- Protect your assets.
- Prepare your financial statements.

By substituting facts for guesswork and continuity for confusion, day-to-day accounting records enable you to keep your finger on the pulse of your business. Any sign of financial ill health can be detected quickly and the appropriate corrective action taken before it's too late.

Business owners sometimes feel that recordkeeping is an unjustifiable waste of time when a good memory is all that's really needed. Unfortunately, memories can fail. Besides, the business owner can't always be around when an employee needs to check an important piece of information. Taking time to set up and maintain your accounting system can actually save time by bringing order out of chaos. Instead of having to hunt for the financial information you need, or develop it on the spot, you already have it in hand, waiting to be used:

- Last month's sales total.
- Sales commissions paid out in the past two weeks.
- Overtime charges for the previous quarter.
- Advertising expenses for the month.
- Percentage of sales made on credit.
- Customers behind on their bills.
- Amount of money tied up in inventory.
- Inventory shortages.
- Slow-moving merchandise.
- Effects of inflation on profits.
- Financial obligations coming due.
- Total value of your assets.

This information, and more, can readily be obtained from an adequate records system. The question isn't whether your business can afford to have one. Rather, it's whether your business can afford *not* to have one.

Accountants. Once the importance of recordkeeping has been recognized, new business owners are often quick to delegate total responsibility for their records to accountants. Pleading ignorance ("What do *I* know about accounting?") or lack of time ("I can either run the business or keep the books."), they dissociate themselves entirely from the accounting function. And why not? After all, that's what accountants are paid for, isn't it? The problem with this tactic is that it gives your accountant free rein to make decisions affecting your business without receiving any input from you. Aside from the fact that this is an open invitation to your accountant to embezzle funds from the business, or use its assets for personal gain, there is an even greater reason for you to keep close tabs on your records system: You can't operate efficiently without access to its information.

For the best results, you and your accountant should work together as a team, supplying each other with accurate and timely information. Whether your accountant handles all your recordkeeping or just does your taxes, it's vital that you understand what is being done.

Setting Up the Books

The first steps in setting up the books for your business is to determine which information to keep and which to discard. A good accounting system gives you only the information you need, not a lot of extraneous details.

Accounts. The foundation on which your recordkeeping system is built is your accounts. Each account represents a single category of business transactions (sales volume, rent expense, employees' wages, cash, notes payable). Any changes (increases or decreases) that occur within a specific category are shown in the appropriate account. In this way, when a sale is made, a bill is paid, or an expense incurred, you have a record of it.

In its simplest form, an account looks like the T account on page 56. All cash flowing into your business is entered on the left side of the cash account. All cash flowing out of your business is entered on the right side. Rather than changing the balance each time cash is added or subtracted, the account mechanism enables you to derive your new balance by simply totaling the two sides and subtracting right from left to get the

T Account

CASH

Increases	Decreases
Beginning Balance $15,000	$600
3,000	250
500	6,350
1,200	
700	
$20,400	$7,200
New Balance $13,200	

difference. This not only saves time, but allows you to see the separate entries that affected the balance.

In comparison to what a regular account looks like, the T account is just the bare outline or skeleton, lacking details. Your actual accounts will probably look something like the accompanying cash account. The basic structure of the T account is still intact, but the refined format enables you to record more information.

Cash Account

ACCOUNT *Cash*   ACCOUNT NO. *101*

DATE		ITEM		DEBIT	DATE		ITEM	CREDIT
19XX Aug.	1	Balance		15 000 00	19XX Aug.	1	Accounts Payable	6 00 00
	2	Sales		3 000 00		2	Supplies	2 50 00

Chart of accounts. As you go through the process of determining which accounting information to keep, the name of each account to be included in your records system should be added to your chart of accounts. This identifies your accounts by title and indicates their locations within the system. For example, the cash account in the illustration shown is numbered 101. This means that it falls under the assets category (arbitrarily assigned the number 10) and is the first account within that section. Depending on the number of accounts you wish to maintain, your numbering system can range from the simple to the sophisticated.

SAMPLE CHART OF ACCOUNTS

(10) *Assets* (Debit)	(30) *Capital Accounts (Credit)*
101—Cash	301—Owners' capital
102—Accounts receivable	302—Undistributed capital
103—Inventory	(40) *Revenues* (Credit)
104—Materials and supplies	401—Retail sales
105—Prepaid expenses	402—Wholesale sales
106—Land	403—Sales—service
107—Buildings	404—Miscellaneous income
108—Reserve for depreciation	
Buildings (Cr)	(50) *Expenses* (Debit)
109—Furniture and fixtures	501—Accounting
110—Reserve for depreciation	502—Advertising
Furniture and fixtures (Cr)	503—Depreciation
111—Automotive equipment	504—Insurance
112—Reserve for depreciation	505—Interest
Automotive equipment (Cr)	506—Miscellaneous
(20) *Liabilities* (Credit)	507—Payroll
201—Accounts payable	508—Rent
202—Notes payable	509—Repairs
203—Sales taxes—payable	510—Supplies
204—FICA taxes—payable	511—Travel
210—Long-term debt—SBA loan	512—Utilities

Double-entry accounting. For every transaction that is recorded, *two* entries are required. This is because any change in one account automatically results in a change in another account. For instance, if a customer purchases merchandise from you and pays cash for it, the balance in your cash account increases and at the same time your merchandise inventory decreases. Both changes must be recorded. The means for doing this is by way of debit and credit entries. In double-entry accounting, for each transaction *the total debit amount must equal the total credit amount.* If for any reason these amounts aren't equal, the transaction has been recorded incorrectly.

How debits and credits work. There are two common misconceptions about debits and credits. One is to think of them as being good things or bad things (as in "the fireman was credited with rescuing the child from the burning building" or "that's one more debit against you"). The other misconception is that "debit" means "to subtract" and "credit" means "to add." Although the outcome of the debit or credit entry can be good or bad and call for addition or subtraction, the terms themselves have much simpler meanings. To debit is to make an entry on the left side of the account. To credit is to make an entry on the right side. Depending on which account is receiving the entry, both debits and credits can be either positive (calling for an increase) or negative (calling for a decrease). The accompanying chart illustrates this.

DEBIT AND CREDIT ENTRIES

Type of Account	To increase the account enter the amount as a	To decrease the account, enter the amount as a
Asset	debit*	credit
Liability	credit*	debit
Capital	credit*	debit
Revenue	credit*	debit
Expense	debit*	credit

*Typical account balance

The accounting process. Entering information into your accounts is neither the first part of the accounting process nor the last. As shown in the chart, the process begins with the business transaction itself and continues until your financial statements have been prepared. Then the cycle begins again.

THE ACCOUNTING PROCESS

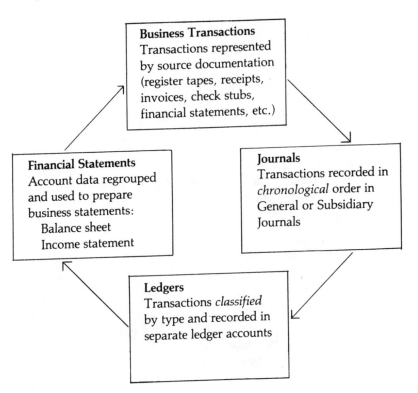

Business Transactions
Transactions represented by source documentation (register tapes, receipts, invoices, check stubs, financial statements, etc.)

Journals
Transactions recorded in *chronological* order in General or Subsidiary Journals

Ledgers
Transactions *classified* by type and recorded in separate ledger accounts

Financial Statements
Account data regrouped and used to prepare business statements:
    Balance sheet
    Income statement

Journals. Once a transaction has occurred, information about it enters your accounting system through your journals. Often called the books of original entry, journals are merely *chronological* records of your business transactions. Each entry contains (1) the date on which the transaction occurred, (2) the specific accounts to be debited and credited, and (3) the amount of the debit and credit.

Although one *general journal* covering all transactions is sometimes sufficient for a small business, the majority of businesses also maintain two additional journals: one for cash receipts and one for cash payments. Keeping separate journals serves three main purposes: (1) it saves time, (2) it saves space, and (3) it reduces errors. These savings stem from the fact that, unlike the general journal, the separate journals offer the following benefits:

1. Headings are preprinted. Thus less time is spent in recording the necessary information.
2. Entries require fewer lines. Thus an entry that takes up three lines in the general journal will require only one line in the cash receipts journal.
3. Column *totals*, rather than separate entries, are transferred later. Reducing the number of entries to transfer also reduces the number of possible errors.

Source documents for journal entries. Each entry that is recorded in your journals must be backed up by the appropriate *source document*—in other words, the written evidence, or business paper, that supports the entry. Examples of source documents are sales receipts, invoices, purchase orders, checks, check stubs, register tapes, credit memos, petty cash slips, and business statements. These are necessary not only for tax reporting purposes, but because they provide an additional safeguard against accounting errors and employee dishonesty.

GENERAL JOURNAL

DATE		ACCOUNT TITLE		DEBIT	CREDIT
1980 NOV.	1	Cash		50 00	
		Office Equipment			50 00
		Receipt No. 1201			
	1	Accounts Payable		325 00	
		Cash			325 00
		Check No. 1151			
	1	Cash		700 00	
		Owners Capital			700 00
		Receipt No. 1202			
	1	Cash		650 00	
		Sales			650 00
		Receipt No. 1203			
	1	Cash		125 00	
		Accounts Receivable			125 00
		Receipt No. 1204			
	2	Rent Expense		725 00	
		Cash			725 00
		Check No. 1152			
	2	Advertising Expense		250 00	
		Cash			250 00
		Check No. 1153			

CASH RECEIPTS JOURNAL

DATE		ACCOUNT TITLE	DOC. NO.	GENERAL 1 DEBIT	GENERAL 2 CREDIT	3 SALES CREDIT	4 ACCOUNTS RECEIVABLE CREDIT	5 CASH DEBIT
1980 NOV	1	Office Equipment	R1201		50 00			50 00
	1	Owners Capital	R1202		700 00			700 00
	1	Sales	R1203			650 00		650 00
	1	Accounts Receivable	R1204				125 00	125 00

CASH PAYMENTS JOURNAL

DATE		ACCOUNT TITLE	Check No.	GENERAL 1 DEBIT	GENERAL 2 CREDIT	3 ACCOUNTS PAYABLE DEBIT	4 CASH CREDIT
1980 NOV	1	Accounts Payable	1151			325 00	325 00
	2	Rent Expense	1152	725 00			725 00
	2	Advertising Expense	1153	250 00			250 00

ACCOUNTS RECEIVABLE CONTROL SHEET

DATE		ITEM	DEBIT	CREDIT	DEBIT BALANCE
1980 Oct	29	Balance			9950 00
	29		150 00		10100 00
	30		300 00	225 00	10175 00
	31			140 00	10035 00
Nov	1			125 00	9910 00

ACCOUNTS RECEIVABLE LEDGER

TERMS 2/10, n/30

NAME Steve Long

ADDRESS 648 Fifth Street   Torrance, Calif.

DATE		ITEM	DEBIT	CREDIT	DEBIT BALANCE
1980 Oct	1	Balance			85 00
	6	Sales Check #345	65 00		150 00
	15	Sales Check #384	50 00		200 00
	21	Sales Check #395	35 00		235 00
	31	Balance			235 00
Nov	1	Received on Account		125 00	110 00

Ledgers. To further consolidate the information contained within your journals and make it more meaningful, the next step in the accounting process is to transfer it to your ledgers. These are the books, files, or even computer discs in which individual accounts are maintained.

All accounts can be grouped together in one general ledger, or, in addition to this, you may want to set up subsidiary ledgers such as an accounts receivable or an accounts payable ledger to house specific categories of high-activity accounts. The advantage is that these subsidiary ledgers make the general ledger less bulky and allow more than one person at a time to work on the ledger accounts. In place of each group of accounts removed from the general ledger a *control sheet*, summarizing the group's activity, is inserted. This enables the general ledger to stay in balance by maintaining the equality of the debits and credits.

The process of transferring the information in the journals to the ledger accounts is called *posting*. During this stage all data of the same kind are separated from the other journal data and entered into their respective accounts. Since the information recorded in each ledger stems from the journals, ledgers are called books of secondary entry.

Financial Statements. Even though your journals alone are sufficient to give you a complete record of your business transactions, without the ledger accounts to categorize that information, it's virtually unusable. To further increase the value of your accounting data, financial statements are also necessary. This is the topic of the next chapter.

Recordkeeping Checklist

To help ensure that your business transactions are properly recorded and measure the effectiveness of your records system, answer the questions in the Recordkeeping Checklist. Any *no* answers indicate areas that need to be examined.

Recordkeeping

Recordkeeping Checklist

	Answer yes or no
1. Do you know the reasons for keeping good records?	_____
2. Have you determined which records are important to your business?	_____
3. Are you using a chart of accounts to show the name and location of each account in your records system?	_____
4. Do you understand the reasoning behind the use of double entry recordkeeping?	_____
5. Is the function of debits and credits clear to you?	_____
6. Can you identify the accounts likely to have debit balances?	_____
7. Can you identify the accounts likely to have credit balances?	_____
8. Have you set up your general journal and any subsidiary journals that will be used?	_____
9. Do you know what source documents are?	_____
10. Is each journal entry made solely on the basis of a source document?	_____
11. Does your filing system enable you to retain and locate all relevant source documents?	_____
12. Have you set up your general ledger and any subsidiary ledgers that will be used?	_____
13. Is information posted to your ledgers periodically?	_____
14. Are all ledger items based on journal entries?	_____
15. Are financial statements prepared at periodic intervals?	_____
16. Do you personally oversee all major business transactions?	_____
17. Are you thoroughly familiar with all aspects of your accounting systems?	_____
18. Does your accounting system enable you to operate your business efficiently and get the full value out of your resources?	_____

19. Are you able to verify the following through your
    records?

    - Cash on hand at the end of the day
    - All money owed to you by customers   _____
    - Accounts that are past due   _____
    - All money owed to suppliers and creditors   _____
    - Bills that have been paid   _____
    - Inventory that has been received   _____
    - Salaries and wages paid   _____
    - All other expenses that have been incurred   _____

20. Have you obtained the advice of an accountant in
    setting up your records system?   _____

Six

—

Financial Statements

The information obtained through your system of financial recordkeeping is only as good as your ability to use it. In addition to compiling your financial data, you must also know how to summarize and interpret it.

Summarizing Financial Data

Summarizing involves taking the information contained within your ledger accounts and using it to prepare the financial statements for your business. The two most important of these are the balance sheet and the income statement (often referred to as a profit and loss statement, or P & L).

The *balance sheet* is a summary of your business's assets, liabilities, and capital on a given day.

The *income statement* is a summary of your business's income and expenses during a specific period (month, quarter, year).

The difference between these statements can be compared to the difference between a photograph and a motion picture.

The balance sheet is like a photograph, depicting your business as it appears in a single instant. The income statement is like a motion picture, depicting your business as it changes over time. Since financial statements are prepared annually (or more often, as desired), it's common to see balance sheets dated "December 31, 19XX" and income statements dated "For the year ended December 31, 19XX."

The Importance of Financial Statements

Unlike day-to-day accounting records, financial statements provide an overview of your business. Instead of telling what you sold on a particular day, or how much a specific inventory item cost, financial statements give you the big picture—comparing what you own to what you owe, what you earned to what you spent. As such, they form the basis for any financial analysis of your business.

Financial statements are absolutely essential for the following:

- *Management planning.* In order to operate your business in the most profitable way possible, or lay the groundwork for future expansion, you need to know where your business stands and how it got there.
- *Raising capital.* Bankers and investors use financial statements as a way of evaluating your business. If you wish to obtain the support of either group, you must not only supply statements, but be ready to explain and defend them.
- *Preparing tax returns.* The information contained within your financial statements is needed in order to prepare your tax returns. Furthermore, in the event of an audit by the Internal Revenue Service, you will be expected to produce the relevant accounting records and statements.

The Balance Sheet

A balance sheet has two main sections, one listing the assets of the business and one listing the liabilities and capital of the business. In accordance with the accounting equation, the two sides are always equal:

$$\text{Assets} = \text{Liabilities} + \text{Capital}$$

This can be readily explained by the fact that all assets in a business are subject to the claims of creditors and owners.

Assets. An asset is anything of monetary value that is owned by the business. Assets are generally classified as being (1) current or (2) fixed or (3) intangible. The order in which they appear on the balance sheet is determined by their *liquidity*—that is their ability to be converted into cash.

Current assets. These consist of cash and assets that are expected to be converted into cash within the coming year. Included in this category are accounts receivable (money owed by customers) and inventory (merchandise, supplies, raw materials, and parts).

Fixed assets. These consist of tangible property to be used over a period of years in operating the business. Included in this category are land, buildings, machinery, equipment, motor vehicles, furniture, and fixtures.

Intangible assets. These consist of items which are usually nonphysical assets. Included in this category are trademarks, patents, copyrights, and goodwill.

Liabilities. A liability is a debt owed by the business. Liabilities are classified as being either current or longterm.

Current liabilities. These consist of debts which are expected to be paid off within the coming year. Included in this category are accounts payable (money owed to suppliers and creditors), notes payable (money owed to the bank), and accrued liabili-

SAMPLE BALANCE SHEET

The Stationery Store
December 31, 19XX
Assets

Current Assets

Cash		$ 5,000	
Accounts Receivable	$12,000		
Less allowance for bad debts	(500)		
		11,500	
Inventory (at cost)		15,500	
Total current assets			$32,000

Fixed Assets

Furniture and fixtures	11,000		
Delivery van	10,000		
		21,000	
Less accumulated depreciation		(1,000)	
Total fixed assets			20,000
Total assets			$52,000

Liabilities and Capital

Current liabilities

Accounts Payable	$9,000		
Notes payable (due within 1 yr.)	4,000		
Accrued liabilities	1,000		
Total current liabilities		$14,000	

Long term liabilities

Notes payable (due after 1 yr.)		4,000	
Total liabilities			$18,000

Capital

Owners capital, January 1, 19XX		33,000	
Net income for year	15,000		
Less proprietor's drawings	(14,000)		
Undistributed income		1,000	
Total capital, December 31, 19XX			34,000
Total liabilities and capital			$52,000

ties (wages, interest, taxes, deposits, and other amounts due but not paid as of the balance sheet date).

Long-term liabilities. These consist of those debts which are *not* due to be paid within the coming year, Included in this category are mortgages, term loans, bonds and similar future obligations.

Capital. The difference between the assets of a business and its liabilities equals it capital:

$$Assets - Liabilities = Capital$$

Capital represents the amount of owner investment in the business, as well as any profits (or losses) that have accumulated.

Sole proprietorship or partnership. In a sole proprietorship or partnership, capital is listed under each owner's name. Increases (or decreases) in capital are also shown there.

Corporation. In a corporation, capital is listed under the heading capital stock. This represents the paid-in value of the shares of stock issued to each owner. Corporate earnings that are not distributed to shareholders are shown here as retained earnings.

The Income Statement

An income statement (or profit and loss statement) can generally be divided into the following sections: net sales, cost of goods sold, gross margin, expenses, and net income (or loss). Together, these demonstrate both the extent and the efficiency of the business's ability to generate income during the accounting period covered by the statement.

Net sales represents the total sales during the accounting period, *less* sales tax and deductions for sales discounts, returns, or allowances.

Cost of goods sold represents the total amount spent by the business to purchase the products sold during the accounting period. Businesses usually compute this by adding the value of

SAMPLE INCOME STATEMENT

The Stationery Store
for the Year Ending December 31, 19XX

			Percent
Net sales		$100,000	100%
Cost of goods sold			
Inventory, January 1		$15,500	
Purchases	$51,100		
Less cash discount	(800)		
		50,300	
Available for sale		65,800	
Less inventory, December 31		(15,800)	
Cost of goods sold		50,000	50
Gross margin		50,000	50
Expenses			
Accounting and legal		1,000	
Advertising		2,500	
Depreciation		1,000	
Insurance		1,000	
Interest		1,000	
Miscellaneous		2,500	
Payroll		12,000	
Rent		8,500	
Repairs		500	
Supplies		1,500	
Travel		2,000	
Utilities		1,500	
Total expenses		35,000	35
Net income		$15,000	15

the goods purchased during the period (less discounts offered by suppliers) to the value of the beginning inventory, and then subtracting the ending inventory.

Gross margin represents the difference between the net sales and the cost of goods sold. It is also frequently referred to as the *gross profit*.

Expenses represent costs which are incurred as a result of operating the business. These can be divided into two categories—*selling expenses* (those expenses, such as sales commissions and advertising, that are directly related to the business's sales activities) and *general and administrative expenses* (those expenses incurred through activities other than selling, such as clerical salaries, rent, and insurance).

Net income represents what's left after all relevant expenses have been deducted from the gross margin. When total expenses exceed the gross margin this is called a *net loss*.

Interpreting Financial Data

Interpreting financial data involves studying the various relationships that exist among the figures shown on your financial statements. These relationships are expressed in the form of *financial ratios*, comparative measurements that enable you to pinpoint the strengths and weaknesses in your business operations.

What if you needed to know the answer to one or more of the following questions?

- Is there enough ready cash in my business?
- Are current liabilities at a safe level?
- How well could the business weather a financial setback?
- Are customers paying their bills on time?
- Is inventory moving as quickly as it should be?
- Are prices keeping pace with inflation?
- Are profits what they should be?
- Are assets being used widely?
- How much of my business do I really own?

How could you get your hands on the necessary information? Call your accountant? Sure, if you had the time and the money to spend waiting for an answer. But why bother when the information is already right at hand, in your financial statements? Solving a few quick arithmetic problems is all it takes to find the answers.

Using financial ratios. Financial ratios can be used to find out a great deal of information about your business, ranging from the trivial to the significant. Among the ratios most closely examined by the owners, investors, and creditors are those pertaining to (1) liquidity, (2) profitability, and (3) ownership.

Liquidity ratios. Measure your business's ability to pay its bills and to convert assets into cash.

Current ratio. This ratio, which compares current assets to current liabilities, is used to assess your business's ability to meet its financial obligations within the coming year. The best known and most widely used of the ratios, it's computed by dividing current assets by current liabilities:

$$\text{Current ratio} = \frac{\text{Current assets}}{\text{Current liabilities}}$$

$$\text{Current ratio} = \frac{\$32,000}{\$14,000}$$

$$\text{Current ratio} = 2.29{:}1$$

The generally acceptable minimum current ratio is 2 to 1. This can vary, though, depending on the specific circumstances of each business.

Acid-test ratio. This ratio, which compares cash and accounts receivable to current liabilities, is used to assess your business's ability to meet its current financial obligations in the event that sales decline and merchandise inventory cannot readily be converted to cash. Also called the *quick ratio* because it measures only ready assets, it's computed by dividing cash and accounts receivable by current liabilities:

$$\text{Acid-test ratio} = \frac{\text{Cash} + \text{Accounts receivable}}{\text{Current liabilities}}$$

$$\text{Acid-test ratio} = \frac{\$5,000 + \$11,500}{\$14,000}$$

Acid-test ratio = 1.2:1

An acid-test ratio of 1 to 1 is considered acceptable, given the fact that an adequate means of collecting accounts receivable exists.

Working capital ratio. This ratio, which compares current assets and current liabilities, is used to assess your business's ability to meet unforeseen expenses or weather a financial setback. It's computed by subtracting current liabilities from current assets:

Working capital = Current assets − Current liabilities
Working capital = $32,000 − $14,000
Working capital = $18,000

Working capital needs vary from business to business. Frequently, though, lenders will insist that the level of working capital be maintained at or above a minimum level.

Average collection period, which compares your average day's sales to accounts receivable, is used to assess your business's ability to convert accounts receivable into cash. It's computed in a two-step process that *first* divides net sales by the number of days in the year; in the *second* step, this figure (the average day's sales) is divided into accounts receivable:

Step 1

$$\text{Average day's sales} = \frac{\text{Net Sales}}{365 \text{ Days}}$$

$$\text{Average day's sales} = \frac{\$100,000}{365}$$

Average day's sales = $274 per day

Step 2

$$\text{Average collection period} = \frac{\text{Accounts receivable}}{\text{Average day's sales}}$$

$$\text{Average collection period} = \frac{\$11,500}{\$274 \text{ per day}}$$

Average collection period = 42 days

What average collection period is acceptable depends on the credit terms. Generally, it should not exceed 1⅓ times the credit terms. Thus, since the Stationery Store offers 30 days credit, its average collection period is slightly higher than it should be (1⅓ × 30 = 40 days).

Inventory turnover compares your cost of goods sold to your average inventory level. Average inventory level is calculated as half the total of beginning inventory plus ending inventory. Inventory turnover is used to assess your business's ability to convert merchandise inventory into sales. It's computed by dividing the cost of goods sold by the average inventory:

$$\text{Inventory turnover} = \frac{\text{Cost of goods sold}}{\text{Average inventory}}$$

$$\text{Inventory turnover} = \frac{\$50,000}{\frac{1}{2}(\$15,5000 + \$15,800)}$$

$$\text{Inventory Turnover} = \frac{\$50,000}{\$15,650}$$

Inventory turnover = 3.2 times

Normally, the higher your turnover is, the better. This means you're moving the goods. However, as the turnover rate increases, so does the risk of stock shortages. By trial and error and by studying the turnover rates of similar businesses, you can determine what rate is desirable for your business.

Profitability ratios. These measure your business's ability to use its assets to make a profit.

Net profit on sales compares net profit to net sales. Used to assess your business's ability to turn a profit on the sales it makes, it's computed by dividing net profit by net sales:

$$\text{Net profit on sales} = \frac{\text{Net profit}}{\text{Net sales}}$$

$$\text{Net profit on sales} = \frac{\$15,000}{\$100,000}$$

$$\text{Net profit on sales} = .15 \text{ or } 15\%$$

In this example, the Stationery Store makes 15 cents profit for every dollar in sales. Whether this is an acceptable level of profit depends on your objectives and the standard for your industry.

Return on investment (ROI) compares net profit to total assets. Used to assess your business's ability to turn a profit on the assets it holds, it's computed by dividing net profit by total assets:

$$\text{Return on investment} = \frac{\text{Net Profit}}{\text{Total assets}}$$

$$\text{Return on investment} = \frac{\$15,000}{\$52,000}$$

$$\text{Return on investment} = .28 \text{ or } 28\%$$

To determine if this is a good return on investment, you should compare your figures to those of comparable businesses.

Ownership ratio measures the levels of ownership in the business, comparing owners' claims to those of creditors.

Worth to debt compares net worth to total debt. It's used to assess your business's ability to protect creditors against losses. To compute it, divide net worth by total debt:

$$\text{Worth to debt} = \frac{\text{Net worth}}{\text{Total debt}}$$

$$\text{Worth to debt} = \frac{\$34,000}{\$18,000}$$

$$\text{Worth to debt} = 1.88:1$$

For every dollar lent to the Stationery Store the owner has invested $1.88. Usually a ratio of 2 to 1 or better is preferred since this provides creditors with more protection. To improve this ratio, the owner can either invest more money in the business or reduce his debt.

Financial Ratio Checklist

Once you have prepared the financial statements for your business, you can pinpoint its financial strengths and weaknesses by computing the ratios in the Financial Ratio Checklist.

FINANCIAL RATIO CHECKLIST

	Ratio	Satis-factory	Unsatis-factory
Liquidity			
Current ratio	___	___	___
Acid-test ratio	___	___	___
Working capital	___	___	___
Average collection period	___	___	___
Inventory turnover	___	___	___
Profitability			
Net profit on sales	___	___	___
Return on investment	___	___	___
Ownership			
Worth to debt	___	___	___

Seven

Obtaining Capital

Prior to commencing operations, you will want to estimate as realistically as possible the amount of capital needed to launch and sustain your business during its first three to six months. This is your initial investment. Since it takes a while before revenues exceed or even equal expenses, a financial cushion is essential in your estimate. The cushion can mean the difference between success and failure, enabling you to meet payroll and supplier obligations, make loan payments, and keep your doors open until the business is fully self-supporting.

A common mistake of first-time entrepreneurs is in neglecting to take into account such invisible costs of operating a business as insurance, deposits or bonds, license fees, estimated sales taxes, and membership dues in professional organizations. If added after the fact, these "incidentals" could easily throw the best of budgets out of kilter.

Your own personal financial needs must also be considered. Not only does your business need capital in order to survive during the first months of operation, but so do you. To be accurate, your estimated initial investment must include an allowance adequate to support yourself while you are establishing your business. This allowance can be in the form of either a salary or drawing account privileges.

Determining Your Initial Investment

For a retail operation. The first step in determining the amount of your initial investment is to estimate your projected annual sales volume. This is based on such factors as the type and size of your intended business and its location. Any previous related business experience that you may have, combined with the most up-to-date research you can find, will be invaluable here. The more you know about your new business, the more you will know what to expect.

Once you have computed your sales volume for the year, it's easy to work backward to figure out the dollar investment necessary to meet your starting merchandise inventory requirements. This is done by dividing estimated sales volume by inventory turnover (the number of times per year that your merchandise will sell out). For instance, if your estimated annual sales volume is $100,000 and you expect to turn over your merchandise three times per year, then your initial merchandise inventory should last four months and have a retail value of $33,333. At cost, given a 50 percent markup, this would amount to an initial investment of $16,667.

Although merchandise inventory turnover varies by industry and by merchandising techniques (high-volume retailer versus specialty store), the average turnover for your type of business can be ascertained by referring to Robert Morris Associates *Statement Studies* or Dun & Bradstreet's *Key Business Ratios*, both available at most libraries. For additional information, make it a point to consult with prospective suppliers too.

Now that you have estimated your initial merchandise inventory costs, the next step is to estimate the amount of money required to meet all other costs during your first turnover period. These include rent, insurance, furniture and fixtures, supplies, salaries, utilities, and advertising. Remember to cushion your projections. When added to your merchandise inventory costs, these will give you the total initial investment required for your business.

INITIAL INVESTMENT FOR A RETAIL OPERATION

Starting inventory at cost		$16,667
Furniture and fixtures		
Purchase price (if paid in full)		4,000
Cash down payment (if purchased on contract)		1,500
Fees for legal, accounting, licenses, and other preopening expenses		1,250
Expenses (for 4 months, 1 turnover period)		
Payroll	$3,000	
Rent	2,800	
Other	5,533	
Total expenses		11,333
Contingencies		1,250
Total initial investment		$36,000

For a non-retail operation. If you are starting a manufacturing company or service establishment, the method of calculating your initial investment will need certain minor revisions. The major difference between a manufacturer and a retailer is that the bulk of the manufacturer's initial investment doesn't go for merchandise; it goes for machinery, which will be used for several years, and for raw materials, which can be converted into finished goods. Furthermore, a manufacturer must make such key decisions as whether to lease equipment and whether to manufacture or purchase the component parts of the product. These decisions will affect the amount not only of your initial investment, but of your taxes as well.

A service establishment, in most cases, requires neither an extensive merchandise inventory nor a large investment in capital equipment. Skills are the main product. As a result, the service establishment is easier to start than either a retailing or manufacturing business and usually calls for a considerably smaller initial investment. This explains in part why the number of businesses categorized as services is increasing at such a rapid rate. Statistics provided by the Labor Department show that service industries will continue to expand and grow for the next ten years.

Sources of Capital

You can turn to a variety of sources in order to obtain financing for your business. Which ones you choose will depend primarily on the way in which the money is to be used in the business and the degree of ownership you wish to retain.

Capital usage. If a large sum of money is required—such as for the purchase of physical facilities, machinery, or inventory —it's likely that you will want to delay repaying this as long as possible. Conversely, smaller sums of money to cover operating expenses would normally be repaid within the year.

Debt versus ownership. Whether you borrow the money you need or solicit it from investors will determine your level of ownership in the business. Once you accept a loan, you have an obligation to repay it with interest. But no ownership is transferred to the lender. Investment capital is just the opposite of this. You neither return the investor's money nor pay interest on it. However, the investor becomes a co-owner with you in the business.

In determining the proper balance of debt capital (borrowed money) to equity capital (invested money) that's right for you, there are two drawbacks of which you should be aware. In the case of debt capital, if for any reason you are unable to repay your loans on time, you could easily be forced into bankruptcy. Equity capital, on the other hand, though seemingly risk-free, presents another problem: control. Unlike lenders, investors have a say in how the business should be run. The greater the amount of equity capital you obtain, the greater the amount of ownership you relinquish.

Personal Investment

Your first and most likely source of capital is of course yourself. The amount of money you decide to invest in starting a business will depend partly on how much money you have readily available, be it in savings, in investments, or paid into your home. It will also depend on how the ownership in the business is to be divided.

Your chances of avoiding investing any of your own money in the business are slim. Since forming a business involves risk, prospective creditors and investors will expect you, the owner, to share in that risk. However, there are exceptions. If you have a unique idea or valuable skills to contribute to the business, these might augment or be an acceptable substitute for capital.

Should you be planning to finance your business solely from your own personal resources, on the other hand, you may want to reconsider. Instead of putting the money directly into the business, it would be to your advantage to use it as collateral for a loan to the business. Not only would this build up your credit standing, but, since the interest paid on the loan is tax-deductible expense, the loan would be virtually cost-free.

Family and Friends

Obtaining money from family and friends, through loans or investments, may also be an alternative. But bear in mind that this can strain both your personal and your business relationships unless the proper safeguards are taken.

The provisions for the repayment of such loans should be clearly stated in writing, including the duration of each loan, the interest rate, and the payment schedule. In this way you can minimize future misunderstandings over the nature of the money entrusted to you.

When relatives or friends become investors in your business the terms of this association should be stipulated in advance. How much of a say will they have in running the business? Do you have the right to buy back their interest in the company? How will the proceeds be distributed? All this should be put in writing. If these questions and others are answered in the beginning, problems may be avoided later.

Partners

Others, besides friends and family, may be interested in entering into the business with you. These could be business acquaintances, classmates, or simply entrepreneurs looking for a business opportunity. Forming a partnership with one or more of these interested parties could be the way to fulfill not only your capital requirements but your personnel needs as well. Remember, though, that in so doing you dilute your ownership and lessen the magnitude of your control.

Shareholders

Selling shares of stock in a business as a means of raising capital is an option permitted only to corporations. Should you decide to do so, you must first incorporate. Since this involves obtaining a corporate charter from the state in which your business will be based, it is advisable to consult an attorney for assistance in this matter.

Offsetting the red tape inherent in forming a corporation is the corporation's unique ability to accumulate large sums of capital. Aided by such features as limited liability and easy transfer of stock ownership, the corporation is able to draw on the resources of a vast and diverse pool of investors. Brought together by a common goal—to make a profit—these investors, as shareholders, will have the right to influence corporate policy decisions. However, you can retain control by holding onto a majority of the shares of stock.

Bondholders

In addition to selling stock, corporations are permitted to sell bonds. Unlike shares of stock, which represent ownership in the business, bonds represent debt. In exchange for investing in bonds, bondholders are paid a predetermined interest rate over the life of the bond. This interest differs from dividends in that it is categorized as a business expense and therefore is deductible. When the bond matures (usually in 10 to 30 years) the bondholder receives the principal investment back.

Since bonds are a form of long-term debt, they are more often used to finance major business expansion costs such as the purchase of plant and equipment. Before making the decision to sell bonds, though, it's important that you determine your corporation's future ability to pay the annual interest and retire the bonds when they reach maturity. Furthermore, during the early stages of your business, investors may be understandably reluctant to purchase the corporation's bonds, preferring that you establish yourself first.

Commercial Banks

Despite what you may have heard about how difficult it is to get a bank loan, banks are a major source of capital for new businesses. Prior to approaching your banker for a loan, though, you should be aware of the criteria on which your request will be evaluated. In banking terminology, there are *six C's of credit.* These are capital, collateral, capability, character, coverage, and circumstances.

Your banker will want to know how much *capital* your business has to start with and what percentage of it is your own personal investment. What assets do you possess that can be used as *collateral* for the loan? Based on your experience and reputation, a determination will be made regarding your *capability* and *character.* The type and amount of insurance *coverage* you plan to obtain is another important factor. The general *circumstances* of your business (competition, level of consumer demand, current economic environment) will also be taken into consideration.

Your ability to sell your banker on your strengths in each of these areas will directly affect the outcome of your loan application. So be prepared to provide such back-up information as financial statements, references, market research data, and a detailed plan for achieving your company's objectives. Establishing your creditworthiness in this way makes it much easier to get a yes answer.

Credit Unions

Another source of funds, similar to a bank, is the credit union. Credit unions offer lower interest rates than banks, but in order to qualify for a loan you must be a member.

Savings and Loan Associations

Savings and loans traditionally make long-term, low-risk loans to home buyers and do not make business loans per se. However, if you are a homeowner it may be possible to get an indirect loan for your business by obtaining a first or second mortgage on your home. In this case, this would be a personal rather than a business loan.

Mortgaging your home can be a risky proposition, since a

business loss could put your home in jeopardy. Furthermore, if a loan is made to you as an individual, rather than to your business, the interest payable on the loan cannot be deducted as a legitimate business expense.

Small Business Administration

The Small Business Administration (SBA) is a federal agency, created in 1953 to provide business with both advice and financial aid. In this regard, it can make either direct or indirect loans to businesses. A direct loan is one made by the SBA itself. An indirect loan is a loan made by another lending institution, but guaranteed up to 90 percent by the SBA. Both kinds have lower interest rates and longer maturities than those associated with conventional loans. But the SBA is not in competition with the financial community. By law, it is permitted to make loans only to applicants who already have been turned down by at least two lending institutions.

In granting loans, the SBA is influenced favorably by the following conditions:

1. The business to be financed is the primary source of income for the family.
2. Financial assistance is not otherwise available on reasonable terms from private sources.
3. A reasonable amount is at stake in the venture. Generally, SBA will want at least 20 percent at stake in a start-up operation.
4. There is reasonable assurance of repayment.
5. The new venture is feasible and sound.
6. The applicant has ability and experience in the area of the business.
7. The applicant is of good character.
8. The borrower agrees not to discriminate in the business on grounds of race, creed, color, or national origin.

Before you attempt to put together a loan application package by yourself, the SBA suggests that you prepare and collect the following information (see forms and questionnaire at the end of this chapter):

1. Business plan.
2. Personal financial statement.
3. Statement of personal history.
4. Start-up costs.
5. Forecast of profit or loss.

Once you have gathered this information, you should contact your local SBA field office to discuss your business plans further. At that point you will receive advice regarding your proposal and the preparation of a loan package.

Small Business Investment Companies

Small Business Investment Companies (SBICs) are privately owned and operated companies that have been licensed and in some cases financed by the Small Business Administration to provide small businesses with long-term debt and equity financing. The intent of the 1958 Small Business Investment Act, authorizing the formation of SBICs, was to increase the number of private companies willing to invest in small businesses.

Though all SBICs must conform to SBA regulations and are subject to SBA control, they are not all the same. SBICs range from those specializing in the entertainment industry to those in the aerospace field. The preferred method of investment (debt vs. equity) and the amount of that investment can also vary. If you are considering SBIC financing, you will therefore want to compare SBICs. To get additional information on SBICs and a list of those near you, contact your local SBA field office.

Supplier Credit

Depending on your credit rating, some suppliers may be persuaded to provide such items as inventory, furniture, fixtures, and equipment on a delayed payment basis. In the case of inventories, full payment would normally be due within 30 days. Furniture, fixtures, and equipment could be paid off over a longer period, perhaps as much as several years.

Supplier credit has two advantages. It allows you to stretch your available cash, and the related interest charges can be deducted from your taxes as business expense. However, since many suppliers offer discounts for early payment, the corresponding disadvantage is that you will be paying higher prices.

Financing Checklist

To get a better idea of the amount of capital you need and to find out if you have thoroughly researched the avenues of financing that are open to you, answer the questions in the Financing Checklist on p. 90.

Financing Checklist

	Answer yes or no
1. Have you determined the amount of initial investment required for your business?	_____
2. Did you include a financial cushion in your esimate?	_____
3. Have you decided how much of your own money to put into the business?	_____
4. Have you weighed the pros and cons and debt versus ownership financing?	_____
5. Have you investigated each of these sources of capital?	
Family	_____
Friends	_____
Partners	_____
Shareholder	_____
Bondholders	_____
Banks	_____
Savings and loan associations	_____
Credit unions	_____
Small Business Administration	_____
SBICs	_____
Suppliers	_____
6. Have you spoken to your banker about obtaining a loan?	_____
7. Would you give yourself a positive rating in each of the six C's of credit?	
Capital	_____
Collateral	_____
Capability	_____
Character	_____
Coverage	_____
Circumstances	_____

FINANCING CHECKLIST (CONT'D)

8. Are you aware of the SBA's criteria for granting
   loans? _____
9. Have you explored the possibility of obtaining
   SBIC financing? _____
10. Have you spoken to an accountant regarding the
    various financing options open to you? _____

SBA BUSINESS PLAN QUESTIONNAIRE

1. Business experience and education?
2. Kind of business? Construction, manufacturing, service . . .etc.
   What is your product? Describe the product or service you plan
   to make or sell.
3. Why did you choose this kind of business?
4. Sole proprietorship, partnership, or corporation?
5. Amount of loan required and anticipated use of funds?
6. Where will the business be located? Why was this location
   selected?
7. How much capital do you have and what will be invested in the
   business (briefly)?
8. Have you attended an SBA Pre-Business Workshop?
9. Do you have an accountant or bookkeeping service in mind to
   set up financial records?
10. What kinds of licensing will you require?
11. How many employees will you need?
12. What kind of insurance will you carry?

PERSONAL FINANCE STATEMENT

Form Approved
OMB No. 100-R-0081

| **PERSONAL FINANCIAL STATEMENT**

As of _____ , 19 ___ . | **Return to:**
Small Business Administration | **For SBA Use Only**

SBA Loan No. |

Complete this form if 1) a sole proprietorship by the proprietor; 2) a partnership by each partner; 3) a corporation by each officer and each stockholder with **20%** or more ownership; 4) any other person or entity providing a guaranty on the loan.

| Name and Address, Including ZIP Code　*(of person and spouse submitting Statement)* | This statement is submitted in connection with S.B.A. loan requested or granted to the individual or firm, whose name appears below:

Name and Address of Applicant or Borrower, Including ZIP Code |

SOCIAL SECURITY NO. _____

Business *(of person submitting Statement)*

Please answer all questions using "No" or "None" where necessary

ASSETS		LIABILITIES	
Cash on Hand & In Banks . . . . $ _____		Accounts Payable . . . . $ _____	
Savings Account in Banks . . . . _____		Notes Payable to Banks. . . . . _____	
U. S. Government Bonds . . . . _____		*(Describe below - Section 2)*	
Accounts & Notes Receivable . . . . _____		Notes Payable to Others. . . . . _____	
Life Insurance-Cash Surrender Value Only . . _____		*(Describe below - Section 2)*	
Other Stocks and Bonds . . . . _____		Installment Account (Auto) . . . . _____	
(Describe - reverse side - Section 3)		Monthly Payments $ _____	
Real Estate . . . . _____		Installment Accounts (Other). . . . . _____	
(Describe - reverse side - Section 4)		Monthly Payments $ _____	
Automobile - Present Value . . . . _____		Loans on Life Insurance . . . . _____	
Other Personal Property. . . . . _____		Mortgages on Real Estate . . . . _____	
(Describe - reverse side - Section 5)		*(Describe - reverse side - Section 4)*	
Other Assets . . . . _____		Unpaid Taxes. . . . . _____	
(Describe - reverse side - Section 6)		*(Describe - reverse side - Section 7)*	
		Other Liabilities. _____	
		(Describe - reverse side - Section 8)	
		Total Liabilities. _____	
		Net Worth . . . . _____	
Total. . . . . $ _____		**Total . . . . $ _____**	

Section 1. Source of Income | **CONTINGENT LIABILITIES**
(Describe below all items listed in this Section)

Salary. . . . . $ _____		As Endorser or Co-Maker . . . . $ _____	
Net Investment Income . . . . _____		Legal Claims and Judgments . . . . _____	
Real Estate Income . . . . _____		Provision for Federal Income Tax . . . . _____	
Other Income *(Describe)* * . . . . _____		Other Special Debt . . . . _____	

Description of items listed in Section 1 _____

_____
_____
_____
_____
_____
_____

* Not necessary to disclose alimony or child support payments in "Other Income" unless it is desired to have such payments counted toward total income.

Life Insurance Held *(Give face amount of policies - name of company and beneficiaries)* _____

_____
_____
_____
_____
_____
_____
_____
_____
_____
_____

SUPPLEMENTARY SCHEDULES

Section 2. Notes Payable to Banks and Others

Name and Address of Holder of Note	Amount of Loan		Terms of Repayments	Maturity of Loan	How Endorsed, Guaranteed, or Secured
	Original Bal.	Present Bal.			
	$	$	$		

Personal Finance Statement (Cont'd)

Section 3. Other Stocks and Bonds: Give listed and unlisted Stocks and Bonds (Use separate sheet if necessary)				
No. of Shares	Names of Securities	Cost	Market Value Statement Date Quotation	Amount

Section 4. Real Estate Owned. *(List each parcel separately. Use supplemental sheets if necessary. Each sheet must be identified as a supplement to this statement and signed). (Also advises whether property is covered by title insurance, abstract of title, or both).*

Title is in name of	Type of property

Address of property (City and State)	Original Cost to (me) (us) $ _____
	Date Purchased _____
	Present Market Value $ _____
	Tax Assessment Value $ _____

Name and Address of Holder of Mortgage (City and State)	Date of Mortgage _____
	Original Amount $ _____
	Balance $ _____
	Maturity _____
	Terms of Payment _____

Status of Mortgage, i.e., current or delinquent. If delinquent describe delinquencies

Section 5. Other Personal Property. *(Describe and if any is mortgaged, state name and address of mortgage holder and amount of mortgage, terms of payment and if delinquent, describe delinquency.)*

Section 6. Other Assets. *(Describe)*

Section 7. Unpaid Taxes. *(Describe in detail, as to type, to whom payable, when due, amount, and what, if any, property a tax lien, if any, attaches)*

Section 8. Other Liabilities. *(Describe in detail)*

(I) or (We) certify the above and the statements contained in the schedules herein is a true and accurate statement of (my) or (our) financial condition as of the date stated herein. This statement is given for the purpose of: (Check one of the following)

☐ Inducing S.B.A. to grant a loan as requested in application, of the individual or firm whose name appears herein, in connection with which this statement is submitted.

☐ Furnishing a statement of (my) or (our) financial condition, pursuant to the terms of the guaranty executed by (me) or (us) at the time S.B.A. granted a loan to the individual or firm, whose name appears herein.

Signature	Signature	Date

United States of America

SMALL BUSINESS ADMINISTRATION

STATEMENT OF PERSONAL HISTORY

Please Read Carefully · Print or Type

Each member of the small business concern requesting assistance or the development company must submit this form in TRIPLICATE for filing with the SBA application. This form must be filled out and submitted.

1. If a sole proprietorship, by the proprietor.
2. If a partnership, by each partner.
3. If a corporation or a development company, by each officer, director, and additionally, by each holder of 20% or more of the voting stock.
4. Any other person including a hired manager, who has authority to speak for and commit the borrower in the management of the business.

Name and Address of Applicant (Firm Name)(Street, City, State and ZIP Code)

SBA District Office and City

Amount Applied for:

1. Personal Statement of: (State name in full, if no middle name, state (NMN), or if initial only, indicate initial). List all former names used, and dates each name was used. Use separate sheet if necessary.

First   Middle   Last

2. Date of Birth: (Month, day and year)

3. Place of Birth: (City & State or Foreign Country)

U.S. Citizen? ☐ yes ☐ no
If no, give alien registration number:

4. Give the percentage of ownership or stock owned or to be owned in the small business concern or the Development Company.

Social Security No.

5. Present residence address
From   To   Address
City   State

Home Telephone No. (Include A/C)
Business Telephone No. (Include A/C)

Immediate past residence address
From   To   Address

BE SURE TO ANSWER THE NEXT 3 QUESTIONS CORRECTLY BECAUSE THEY ARE IMPORTANT.

THE FACT THAT YOU HAVE AN ARREST OR CONVICTION RECORD WILL NOT NECESSARILY DISQUALIFY YOU, BUT AN INCORRECT ANSWER WILL PROBABLY CAUSE YOUR APPLICATION TO BE TURNED DOWN.

6. Are you presently under indictment, on parole or probation?
☐ Yes ☐ No   If yes, furnish details in a separate exhibit. List name(s) under which held, if applicable.

7. Have you ever been charged with or arrested for any criminal offense other than a minor motor vehicle violation?
☐ Yes ☐ No   If yes, furnish details in a separate exhibit. List name(s) under which charged, if applicable.

8. Have you ever been convicted of any criminal offense other than a minor motor vehicle violation?
☐ Yes ☐ No   If yes, furnish details in a separate exhibit. List name(s) under which convicted, if applicable.

9. Name and address of participating bank

The information on this form will be used in connection with an investigation of your character. Any information you wish to submit, that you feel will expedite this investigation should be set forth.

Whoever makes any statement knowing it to be false, for the purpose of obtaining for himself or for any applicant, any loan, or loan extension by renewal, deferment or otherwise or for the purpose of obtaining, or influencing SBA toward, anything of value under the Small Business Act, as amended, shall be punished under Section 16(a) of that Act, by a fine of not more than $5000, or by imprisonment for not more than 2 years, or both.

Signature   Title   Date

It is against SBA's policy to provide assistance to persons not of good character and therefore is given to the qualities and personality traits of a person, favorable and unfavorable, relating thereto, including behavior, integrity, candor and disposition toward criminal actions. It is also against SBA's policy to provide assistance not in the best interests of the United States, for example, if there is reason to believe that the effect of such assistance will be to encourage or support, directly or indirectly, activities inimical to the Security of the United States. Anyone concerned with the collection of this information, as to its voluntariness, disclosure or routine uses may contact the FOIA Office, 1441 "L" Street, N.W., and a copy of 9 "Agency Collection of Information" from SOP 40 04 will be provided.

SBA FORM 912 (3-79) SOP 50 10 1 EDITION OF 5-78 WILL BE USED UNTIL STOCK IS EXHAUSTED.

1. SBA FILE COPY

SBA START-UP COSTS FORM

Whether you are starting a new business, moving to a new location, opening a new branch, or expanding your business, you will have some "start-up" or one time expenses. In all applications for such purposes, the following information will be required:

1. Furniture, fixtures, machinery, equipment:
   a. Purchase Price (if paid in full with cash) $_____
   b. Cash Down Payment
      (if purchased on contract) $_____
   c. Transportation and Installation Costs $_____

2. Starting Inventory and Supplies $_____

3. Decorating/Remodeling/Leasehold
   Improvements $_____

4. Deposits
   a. Utilities $_____
   b. Rents/Leases $_____
   c. Other (identify) $_____

5. Fees
   a. Legal, Accounting, Other $_____
   b. Licenses, Permits, etc. $_____
   c. Other (identify) $_____

6. Other (Working Capital, etc.) $_____

                              TOTAL $_____

      Less Equity Injection $_____

      Amount of Loan Request $_____

FORECAST OF PROFIT/LOSS

	1st Month	2nd Month	3rd Month	4th Month	5th Month	6th Month	7th Month	8th Month	9th Month	10th Month	11th Month	12th Month	Total Year
1. TOTAL SALES (Net)													
2. COST OF SALES													
3. GROSS PROFIT (line 1 minus line 2)													
4. EXPENSES (operating)													
5. SALARIES (other than owner)													
6. PAYROLL TAXES													
7. RENT													
8. UTILITIES (incl. phone)													
9. INSURANCE													
10. PROFESSIONAL SERVICES (i.e., acct.)													
11. TAXES AND LICENSES													
12. ADVERTISING													
13. SUPPLIES (for business)													
14. OFFICE SUPPLIES(forms, postage,etc.)													
15. INTEREST (on loans, contracts, etc.)													
16. DEPRECIATION													
17. TRAVEL (incl. operating costs of veh.)													
18. ENTERTAINMENT													
19. DUES & SUBSCRIPTIONS													
20. OTHER													
21.													
22. TOTAL: EXPENSES (add lines 5 thru 21)													
23. PROFIT BEFORE TAXES (line 3 minus 22)													

Eight

Controlling Your Inventory

Every business, regardless of whether its primary function is retailing, wholesaling, services, or manufacturing, has one thing in common—inventory. In fact, the major portion of your investment dollars is likely to go for inventory. Included in this are expenditures for merchandise, supplies, raw materials, and parts, all of which are expected to earn profits for your business. To do so, however, they must be kept in proper balance. This is the aim of inventory control.

A good inventory control system does four things:

1. It keeps inventory at the optimum level.
2. It orders goods in the most economical quantities.
3. It speeds up merchandise turnover.
4. It reduces inventory shrinkage.

In other words, it enables you to get maximum value out of your inventory at minimum cost. But if it can do all that it must be complicated, right? Not really. Actually, it's pretty simple. Just as a thermostat is keyed to react to changes in temperature, an inventory control system reacts to changes (or the lack of changes) in your level of inventory. Once you've set up the system, it's almost totally automatic.

The Optimum Level of Inventory

Many businesses mistakenly abide by the philosophy that the more inventory you have on hand, the better, as a way of making sure that no sales are lost. What they don't realize is that the costs of carrying the extra inventory could more than equal the "profits" from the additional sales. Added to the cost of the inventory itself are the costs of shipping, storage, insurance, and taxes. And there's always the danger that the inventory will become obsolete before it can be used or sold. That's a high price to pay for the security of having your shelves full.

Adopting a let-them-eat-cake attitude isn't the solution either. Purposely letting your business run short on the inventory used for operations activities or sales is guaranteed to alienate customers and employees alike. Among the costs incurred as a result of inventory shortages are special handling charges and sacrificed purchase discounts, because of the need to place rush orders; underutilization of personnel, equipment, and facilities; and lost sales. When sales are involved, your loss can be far-reaching. This is because dissatisfied customers have a tendency to take their future business elsewhere.

This brings us to your objective—the optimum level of inventory. What is it? It's the level of inventory that is the most profitable. Rather than eliminating the costs of stock shortages altogether, or reducing inventory carrying costs to the lowest possible figure, it results in the lowest *total* of the two.

For example:

Inventory level	Costs of stock shortages	Costs of extra inventory	Total
A	$1,000	$8,750	$9,750
B	$2,500	$6,500	$9,000
C	$3,750	$4,000	$7,750
D	$5,500	$3,000	$8,500

The optimum level at which to maintain inventory is level C, since this reduces the total cost by the greatest amount.

Once you've established, through trial and error, the optimum level of inventory for your business, it's up to your control system to keep it at that level. This is accomplished by (1) measuring the goods on hand, (2) indicating the amounts needed, and (3) calculating delivery times.

Measuring the goods on hand. This is the way to find out what you have and what you don't have. Does that carton on the top shelf contain a dozen widgets, as marked, or is it empty? There are three ways to find out: make an educated guess, open the carton and count what's inside, or check your records.

1. *Educated guess.* This method relies on your memory and powers of observation to determine what's in stock. In the event that your business is small and you're able to keep close tabs on the day-to-day operations, it might be fairly accurate. But there's also a good chance it could be wrong. To be on the safe side, you should do a physical count at least once a year.

2. *Physical count.* The most accurate, albeit time-consuming, way to monitor your inventory levels is to do a physical count. This means tallying the goods on hand at periodic intervals to make sure that your estimated inventory matches up with your actual inventory.

3. *Perpetual inventory.* A perpetual inventory system records changes in stock as they occur. Using the information obtained from stock tags, receipts, and requisition forms, the

appropriate stock number, size, color, and so on are entered into the inventory filing system at the time the goods are received, used, or sold. This can be done manually or by computer. When using this system, supplement it with a physical count one or more times per year. (See the perpetual inventory file card.)

PERPETUAL INVENTORY FILE CARD

| Description_____ Location _____ |
| Supplier _____ Reorder point _____ |
| EOQ _____ |

Received		Sold		Balance	
Date	Amount	Date	Amount	Date	Amount

Indicating the amounts needed. Having determined the extent of your inventory, you've reached the crucial point in the control process—deciding what to order and how much. This is where the automatic feature of your inventory control system comes into action. Based on your estimates of the minimum quantities of goods that are required to keep your inventory in balance, the system is programmed to react to specific *reorder points*. Each reorder point represents the level at which an inventory item needs to be replenished. The actual amount

to be purchased is determined by such information updates
as—

- Changes in operations activities.
- Changes in customer preferences.
- Changes in seasons.
- Changes in products (improved, discontinued, and so on).
- Changes in profit margins.
- Changes in suppliers.

For instance, if the customer demand for a particular item is
starting to taper off, you might decide to let that item drop
below its reorder point without purchasing additional stock.

Calculating delivery times. The success of your inventory
control system hinges on your ability to calculate delivery
times. How long will it take the supplier to fill your order—not
just to verify it over the phone, but actually process the paperwork, pack the goods, and deliver them to your place of business? Unless the goods are on your shelves when you need
them, not merely somewhere in transit, your hope of maintaining a balanced inventory is slight.

The way to minimize foul-ups in deliveries is to maintain
good supplier relations. This means familiarizing yourself with
each supplier's delivery capabilities (lead time needed, special
order policy, dependability, and so on) so that you know what
to expect. It also means keeping your requests within reason
(not "I need it yesterday"). When suppliers find that you have
an understanding of their business operations, they are more
inclined to take an interest in yours. If this policy fails and you
get poor service, don't be afraid to switch suppliers.

Economic Order Quantity

In addition to keeping your inventory at the optimum level,
it's the function of your control system to determine the *economic order quantity* for each item. This is the number of units
you must order so as to achieve the lowest total cost. Using

your reorder points and estimated demand levels as a spring-
board, you already know what to order and how much. And
you know the delivery capabilities of your suppliers. But
should you place one large order? Several small orders? A few
medium-sized orders? What's the most economical order
quantity?

INVENTORY ORDERING CYCLE

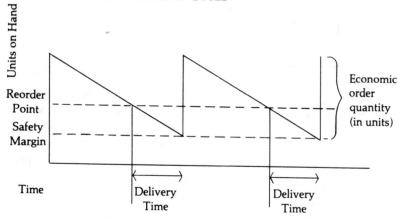

The economic order quantity can be arrived at by offsetting
the costs associated with each order. For instance, the larger
your order, the greater your inventory carrying costs, but the
smaller your ordering and delivery costs. Conversely, with
small orders your carrying costs decrease, and delivery costs
go up.

At first, coming up with a winning combination might seem
a little like trying to balance on a teeter-totter . . . by yourself.
Fortunately, there's a formula that you can use to calculate the
right answer:

–Economic order quantity $= \sqrt{\dfrac{2SC}{IP}}$

Where: S = Sales (in units) for the period
         C = Cost of ordering (clerical, shipping, etc.)

$$I = \text{Inventory carrying charge (storage, insurance, taxes), expressed as a percent of inventory value}$$

$$P = \text{Price per unit}$$

Thus if: $S = 5,000$ units
$C = \$50$
$I = 15\%$
$P = \$25$

$$EOQ = \sqrt{\frac{2SC}{IP}}$$

$$EOQ = \sqrt{\frac{2 \times 5,000 \times \$50}{.15 \times \$25}}$$

$$EOQ = \sqrt{\frac{\$500,000}{\$3.75}}$$

$$EOQ = \sqrt{133,333}$$

$$EOQ = 365 \text{ units}$$

The hardest part of ascertaining the EOQ is figuring out the square root at the end. But don't let that discourage you from using the formula. An electronic calculator or square root table can solve the problem. Furthermore, once you have determined the economic order quantity for a specific item, it isn't necessary to recalculate it each time you order unless there are changes in demand, costs, or delivery capabilities.

Purchase discounts. In calculating the economic order quantities of the inventory items you need, it's important to pay close attention to purchase discounts. These are price reductions made available by suppliers on the basis of order size, total purchases per period, order season, or credit terms.

1. *Order size.* A discount is given when a larger order is placed. This encourages customers to order in larger quantities, thus reducing the supplier's shipping and handling costs, while increasing revenues.

2. *Total purchases.* A discount is given as the total amount of your purchases per period increases. This is done to stimulate repeat buying.

3. *Order season.* A discount is given when your order is placed prior to the peak ordering season. In this way suppliers can even out demand levels and reduce storage requirements.

4. *Credit terms.* A discount is given when prompt payment is made for goods that have been received. The most commonly offered discount is 2/10, net 30. This authorizes you to deduct 2 percent from your bill if payment is made within ten days; otherwise you are expected to pay the full amount in thirty days.

By taking advantage of these discounts, you can further reduce your ordering costs. However, this doesn't mean that you should purchase more than you need or can afford in an effort to save money. Each inventory item purchased should be justified on its own merits, exclusive of any accompanying discounts.

Merchandise Turnover

Your inventory control system can help you speed up merchandise turnover in a variety of ways. These include:

- Improving purchasing methods.
- Monitoring inventory levels.
- Identifying hard-to-move items.
- Adjusting for seasonal demand.
- Recognizing trends.

Rather than waiting till you're stuck with an oversupply of any one item, an effective system alerts you to the potential inventory problem before it happens. This enables you to stay on top of things by cutting back orders if necessary, modifying display and sales techniques, reducing markups, or increasing promotional efforts.

Inventory Shrinkage

Inventory shrinkage refers to unaccountable stock shortages. Inventory that should be in your stockroom or on your shelves may just disappear. This can be caused by employee or customer theft, misplaced stock, or simply poor recordkeeping. Whatever the reason, missing inventory can be a source of frustration and mystification to the business owner, who often feels powerless to stop it.

One way to combat shrinkage is to tighten security. But the effectiveness of this method will be diluted unless it is backed up by inventory control. To reduce shrinkage, the following inventory controls are recommended:

- Inventory shipments should be logged in when received.
- Purchase orders and invoices should be properly filed.
- Requisition forms should be used to keep track of the supplies, materials, and parts used in operating your business.
- A record should be kept of all sales transactions.
- A physical inventory should be taken at least once each year.
- Perpetual inventory figures should be matched against physical inventory results.

These will help you to prevent most inventory shrinkage from occurring and to detect it quickly when it does occur.

Inventory Checklist

To find out whether your inventory control system is doing all the things it's supposed to do, answer the questions in the Inventory Checklist on p. 106.

INVENTORY CHECKLIST

	Answer yes or no
1. Do you have an adequate system for monitoring your level of inventory?	_____
2. Is a physical count taken at least once a year?	_____
3. Have you determined the optimum level of inventory for your business?	_____
4. Have you established reorder points for replenishing inventory items?	_____
5. Do you make adjustments for changes in customer demand when placing orders?	_____
6. Are you familiar with suppliers' delivery capabilities?	_____
7. Do you order in the most economic quantities?	_____
8. Do you take advantage of purchase discounts?	_____
9. Do you keep track of slow-moving stock?	_____
10. Can you spot potential fast movers?	_____
11. Is your merchandise inventory balanced by price line, color, size, and type?	_____
12. Do you select merchandise items with your target customers in mind?	_____
13. Are you taking preventive action against inventory shrinkage?	_____
14. Is your inventory as profitable as it should be?	_____

Nine

Setting the Price

In setting the prices for your products and services, among the factors that have to be considered are the reactions of your customers, the stiffness of the competition, and the state of the economy. Strange as it may seem, a price that's too low can be just as much of a turn-off to customers as a price that's too high. Low prices are often interpreted as signifying low value or inferior merchandise. As for the competition, since your business doesn't exist in a vacuum, the role of other businesses in influencing your prices has to be recognized. Whether you decide to go head-to-head with competitors on prices, matching them dollar for dollar, or to undercut them, or to charge higher prices is crucial to your pricing. Nor can the state of the economy be overlooked. Unemployment, inflation, interest rates, government policies, and levels of investment all have an effect on consumer spending and therefore on your prices.

You must also take into consideration another factor—profit. If your prices are so low that they fail to cover your expenses, or so high that an insufficient number of people wants to buy from you, the result is a loss of profits. Your goal is to meet the demands of customers, keep an eye on competitors and the economy, and assure yourself of satisfactory profits.

Pricing and Customers

Part of knowing what prices to charge comes from knowing your customers. One customer's bargain may be another's extravagance. Affluent customers generally demand high-quality merchandise, personalized service, and an exclusive and attractive environment in which to shop. In exchange for these amenities, they are not only willing to pay more, but *expect* to pay more. Low-income customers, on the other hand, are primarily concerned with stretching their dollars. They're willing to settle for less quality and service and a no-frills, discount house type of environment in exchange for lower prices. In each case the price is what counts.

In the beginning, formulating a price strategy to please your customers may seem like trying to solve the riddle of the chicken and the egg. Which comes first? Should you set your prices and then wait for your target customers to find you? Or should you wait to see what kind of customers you attract, and then develop an appropriate pricing strategy? The answer is both. To a great extent your pricing strategy will be predetermined by your type of business, location, target customers, expenses, and so on. But you also have to stay in touch with your customers to make sure that your prices, quality, and service continue to reflect their needs and wants.

Pricing and Competition

Keeping tabs on competitors' prices helps you to assess your own pricing strategy. Are yours higher or lower than the competition? If your prices are higher, you're probably losing out on sales. If your prices are lower, you may be making more sales but passing up additional profits. In comparing your prices with the competition, don't forget to compare service as well. Services add to the value of a product and therefore to its price. Such services as a prestige location, attractive facilities, personal attention, credit, gift wrapping, validated parking, warranties, and home deliveries benefit your customers. The more services you provide, the higher your prices are likely to be.

Here are some of the sources of information you can use to stay in touch with competitors' pricing strategies.

Customers. Observing customers' shopping habits and listening to what they have to say can give you a pretty good idea of how your prices stack up against the competition.

Suppliers. Since *your* suppliers are also *their* suppliers, this is another source of competitive information. But don't forget that the information flows both ways. Your competitors can tap into the same source to find out about you.

Advertising. Following competitors' promotional campaigns enables you to keep track of pricing changes and also obtain current information about the quality and service being provided.

Competitors' catalogs and price lists. When these are available, they are an excellent source of information, particularly since the prices are not only current but conveniently arranged for easy reference.

Price checkers. These are shoppers employed by you to go out and gather information about competitors' prices. While pretending to shop, they actually record the prices of various key items.

Pricing and the Economy

Customer shopping habits reflect the state of the economy. During a recession or depression, customers are at their most price-conscious. Worried about the high cost of living, threats of unemployment, and cutbacks in credit, they want to make every dollar count. As the economy improves, customers become more optimistic about the future and are more willing to pay higher prices. When the economy is at its peak and business is booming, customers offer little resistance to rising prices. The general feeling is that there's more money where that came from, so why not spend it?

As a business owner, your ability to recognize these fluctuations in the economy and to adjust your prices accordingly adds to your competitiveness. To keep your prices in line with customers' expectations you may add or drop services, raise or lower quality standards, change your markups, or a combination of these.

Pricing and Profit

Your prices should be set at a level sufficient to reimburse you for the cost of the goods or services sold, cover your overhead costs, and provide a profit. The amount of profit you receive will be dependent on your gross margin, or *markup*. This is the difference between the cost and the selling price of the goods sold. The higher the markup, the greater your profit *per sale*. However, this doesn't necessarily mean that your overall profits will be higher. Why? Because higher markups usually result in reduced sales. This explains why discount stores are able to make healthy profits despite lower than average markups; their sales volume is higher.

Pricing Methods

There are a number of pricing methods to choose from, ranging from the simple to the complex. Here are three of the most used methods.

1. *Competitive pricing.* Prices are set at or below the competition's. Costs are made to conform to the prices that have been set.

2. *Standard markup pricing.* A standard markup is computed and then added to the cost of the goods or services sold.

Some businesses apply a single markup across the board, while others have different markups for each sales category.

3. *Cost-oriented pricing.* Prices are set individually, based on the cost of the goods or services sold, the overhead, and the desired profit.

Of the three methods, cost-oriented pricing is the most accurate but also the most complex and time-consuming, since each product or service is evaluated separately. A standard markup saves time by eliminating the need to do individual computations. For a store that carries hundreds or thousands of merchandise items, this can make a big difference. Competitive pricing is the simplest method of all. Prices are virtually preset, being based on what's acceptable for your industry.

Common sense and a little experimentation will soon tell you which method or combination of methods works best for you. If you're in a highly competitive industry where the key determinant of sales is the price, you'll have little choice but to use the competitive pricing method. For businesses with extensive inventories, time considerations alone will dictate that some sort of standardized markup be used. The cost-oriented pricing method is normally used by businesses offering one-of-a-kind products or specialized services.

More About Markups

In computing markups, if you aren't careful you can easily shortchange yourself. A common mistake among new business owners is to forget to include all relevant expenses in the final figure. As a result, potential profits are eaten up and sometimes even converted into losses. Your markup needs to cover all administrative expenses, all selling expenses, and all losses stemming from merchandise discounts, theft, or damage. In addition, it has to provide a measure of profit.

This holds true regardless of which pricing method you use. In the standard markup method, these cost and profit considerations are all built into the markup figure itself. With cost-oriented pricing, they are added as you go. And in competitive pricing you work backward from the price to figure the markup.

Markup to price. You can determine what your selling price would be, given a particular markup, by using this formula:

$$\text{Selling price} = \frac{\text{Cost of goods or services}}{100 - \text{Markup}} \times 100$$

For instance, if a man's suit cost $60 and your markup is 50 percent, you would calculate the selling price as follows:

$$\text{Selling Price} = \frac{\$60}{100 - 50} \times 100$$

Selling price = $120

Price to markup. If you're considering a particular price and want to know what the amount of your markup would be, you can figure that out too:

$$\text{Markup} = \frac{\text{Selling price} - \text{Cost}}{\text{Selling price}}$$

Using the cost and selling price from the previous example, the markup would be calculated like this:

$$\text{Markup} = \frac{\$120 - \$60}{\$120}$$

$$\text{Markup} = \frac{\$60}{\$120} = 50\%$$

Pricing Strategy

Now that you have the basics, it's time to consider strategy. If pricing were just a matter of plugging different numbers into

a formula and coming up with the right figure, it wouldn't require any strategy at all—just a good head for numbers. This
isn't the case. In addition to mathematical ability, you need
marketing savvy.

Elasticity. The first thing you need to find out is how respon-
sive your market is to a change in price. This responsiveness is
called *elasticity.* Products such as eggs, baking soda, razor
blades, and medicine are highly *inelastic.* Regardless of
whether their prices are raised or lowered, customers continue
to purchase them in approximately the same quantities. Customer demand for *elastic* products, on the other hand, fluc-
tuates with the price. A small change in price—up or down—
results in an increase or decrease in the number of units sold.
Television sets, strawberries, clothing, and record albums are
highly elastic.

As a rule, items that are considered to be necessities are less
elastic than those that are considered to be luxuries. This is because the customer's need, rather than the product's price, trig-
gers the purchase. For instance, a person with a headache
doesn't wait until aspirin is on sale before buying it. The need
to get rid of the headache takes priority over the price.

How does all this affect your pricing strategy? Well, for one
thing, the more inelastic your product is, the easier it is to raise
your prices without hurting your sales. That means more profits on the same volume. To increase your profits on highly
elastic products, rather than raising your prices you might try
lowering them. Although this reduces your profit on each unit
sold, the resultant increase in sales volume should increase
your overall profits.

Other Determinants of Price

In addition to product elasticity, other pricing determinants
include the following:

Volume. Are you selling to a mass market or just an elite

few? High-volume businesses generally employ low markups. Conversely, the lower your volume is, the higher the markup you'll need in order to cover your overhead and provide a profit.

Image. Do you want your business known for its quality or for having the best buys? If you're after a quality image, you may decide to use a *prestige* pricing strategy. This strategy calls for deliberately setting prices high in order to attract affluent customers. The opposite of prestige pricing is *leader* pricing. Used to draw large numbers of customers into a store, leader pricing emphasizes low-priced specials that have common appeal. Two-for-one sales and cents-off coupons are typical of this.

Customer psychology. According to market researchers, consumers react more favorably to certain prices than others. An item selling for $9.95 or even $9.99 has a better chance of being purchased than the identical item at $10. Even though the difference in price is insignificant, psychologically it makes a difference.

Product life span. What's the life span of your product? If you're selling fashion or *fad* items (string bikinis, pet rocks) that appeal to customers for only a brief time, you need to make your profits quickly. Otherwise, you could be left holding a bagful of expenses when the demand drops off. The longer your product's life span, the longer the period of time you have in which to earn your profits. This explains the numerous claims by advertisers that their products are new and improved. For the most part, such assertions are nothing more than attempts to stretch a product's life span and extend profits.

Profit objectives. In formulating pricing strategy, the key thing to remember is not to lose sight of your overall objective —maintaining profitability. This may mean taking a loss on one product to stimulate the sales of another (leader pricing). It can also call for changes in your method of operation (high volume vs. low volume). Just as your business doesn't exist in a vacuum, neither do your pricing decisions. Price is only one of the four components that make up the *marketing mix*. The others—product, place, and promotion—must all be in harmony with the prices you set. The products and services you decide to sell, your distribution system, and the messages you communicate about your business directly influence your pricing strategy and profitability.

Pricing Strategy Checklist

For help in developing your pricing strategy and keeping it on target, answer the questions in the Pricing Strategy Checklist. Afterward, compare your answers to see if there are any inconsistencies in your overall pricing strategy.

PRICING STRATEGY CHECKLIST

	Answer yes or no
1. Do you try to evaluate the market forces affecting the demand for your products?	_____
2. Have you considered what price strategies would be compatible with your total marketing mix?	_____
3. Do you know which products are slow movers and which are fast?	_____
4. Do you know which products are elastic and which are inelastic?	_____
5. Do you know your competitors' pricing strategies?	_____
6. Are you influenced by competitors' price changes?	_____
7. Do you regularly review competitors' ads to update your information on their prices?	_____
8. Is your store large enough to employ a comparison shopper?	_____
9. Is there a specific time of year when your competitors have sales?	_____

Pricing Strategy Checklist (cont'd)

		Answer yes or no
10.	Do your customers expect sales at certain times?	_____
11.	Would periodic special sales, combining reduced prices and heavier advertising, be consistent with the store image you are seeking?	_____
12.	Should any leader offerings (selected products with quite low, less profitable prices) be used?	_____
13.	Will cents-off coupons be used in newspaper ads or mailed to selected consumers on any occasion?	_____
14.	Will odd-ending prices, such as $9.95 or $9.99, be more appealing to your customers than even-ending pricing?	_____
15.	Have you determined whether to price below, at, or above the market?	_____
16.	Do you determine specific markups for each product?	_____
17.	Do you use standardized markups for product categories?	_____
18.	Are your prices set so as to cover the full costs on every sale?	_____
19.	Are additional markups called for, because of increases, or because an item's low price causes consumers to question its quality?	_____
20.	Should employees be given purchase discounts?	_____
21.	Should any group of customers, such as students or senior citizens, be given purchase discounts?	_____

Ten

Staffing

The most valuable asset of any business is its people. Land, buildings, merchandise, and equipment may dominate a balance sheet, but they don't make a business successful; people do. The best businesses are the ones that have the best people—capable, creative, energetic people. To attract them requires both ingenuity and initiative on your part. But the payoff in productivity is worth it. Staffing your business with the best people available should be one of your highest priorities.

Placing a sign in your window saying, "Help wanted, apply within" is one way to get results. But not necessarily the results you want. A sign in the window will probably bring in a stream of applicants. But unless they possess the skills to do the job, a great deal of time can be wasted in interviewing and you still would not find anyone you want to hire. Generally, the sign in the window works only when the position to be filled calls for little or no skills and entails a minimum amount of responsibility. How then should you go about hiring the people you need? First it's important to realize that hiring is only one element in staffing. This is an ongoing process that involves finding qualified people, hiring them, making the best use of their skills and abilities, and having them stay on the job instead of quitting and taking their talents elsewhere.

The steps you must take *before* you hire anyone are to (1) analyze each job, (2) prepare job descriptions, (3) check recruitment sources, (4) utilize application forms, (5) conduct interviews, and (6) verify information. *After* the hiring decision is made you have to (1) provide job orientation, (2) provide training, (3) evaluate performance, (4) compensate employees, and (5) monitor employee turnover. By following these steps, instead of waiting for fate to send you perfect employees or complaining about your current employees, you can control and direct the staffing process.

Analyze Each Job

This is the most important step in staffing since it forms the basis for any hiring decisions that you make. Unfortunately, it's often skipped over by employers who, in a rush to get a position filled quickly, would rather hire now and ask questions later. Then, when confronted with poor performance, low morale, and high turnover, they wonder why it's so hard to find good workers any more. Taking a little more time in the beginning is the way to avoid a great many problems later.

During the job analysis step your should ask yourself:

- What work has to be accomplished?
- Do I need additional help to do it?
- How many people do I need?
- Would part-time help be sufficient?
- What skills am I looking for?
- How much experience is required?
- Is the labor market favorable?
- How much am I able to pay?

You may find that you don't need to hire anyone after all. Perhaps, if you reschedule the work flow or juggle work assignments, your present staff can handle it. Or you may find out that one additional person isn't enough. Maybe you need to hire two or more people to keep pace with the workload. Or a job you thought anyone can do may in fact require someone with specific skills. The answer to your questions can be surprising. But that's the point of doing a job analysis. It's better to be surprised before you hire someone, rather than after. The choice is yours. You can be the one saying, "If only I'd known," or you can take the time to find out.

Prepare Job Descriptions

A job description is a written record of the duties and responsibilities associated with a particular job. It serves a dual purpose, making it easier for you to match the right person to the right job and informing each employee of what his/her job entails.

In preparing a job description, include the following details:

- A general description of the job.
- The duties to be performed.
- The job responsibilities.
- Specific skills needed.
- Education and experience required.

For instance, a receiving clerk in a store might have a job description that looks like the sample shown on page 120. Once you've put everything down on paper, you're ready to start looking for the person who fits the description.

Check Recruitment Sources

The method of recruitment that you decide to utilize depends on your business. Waiters and waitresses might easily be recruited from your local high school. Finding qualified real estate brokers or skilled carpenters calls for a different method. Some of the sources available for you to choose from are the following:

SAMPLE JOB DESCRIPTION

Job Title: Receiving clerk

Supervisor: Store owner

Summary: Responsible for receiving shipments from suppliers. Removes goods from containers and places them on warehouse shelves. Prepares and processes paperwork and maintains receiving files.

Duties and responsibilities:

- Removing stock from containers and placing merchandise on warehouse shelves.
- Checking invoices to merchandise received.
- Inspecting merchandise received.
- Typing miscellaneous forms and labels.
- Maintaining receiving files.
- Assisting in physical inventory.
- Keeping warehouse clean and orderly.

Job Specificiations:

- Education: High school graduate
- Experience: None required
- Skills: Must be able to organize material; work with numbers; interact well with people.

Public employment agencies. Public employment agencies operate throughout each state, finding and placing both blue collar and white collar workers. Without charge, they will recruit and screen job applicants, sending you only the ones who meet your specifications.

Private employments agencies. Private employment agencies operate much the same as public ones do, except that there is a fee involved. Either you pay it or the person who is hired pays it.

Newspaper advertisements. A newspaper advertisement enables you to reach a large pool of interested job applicants quickly. However, it's important to design your ad in such a way as to attract those who are qualified, while discouraging the unqualified. The way to do this is to: (1) make it interesting, (2) give adequate details about the job, (3) indicate the skills needed, and (4) specify the education and experience. A general guideline is to stick to a straightforward approach, since cute or exaggerated copy tends to generate a negative reaction.

Local schools. Contacting the placement centers at local high schools and colleges is a good way to find applicants who are long on potential, though usually short on experience. If you're looking for part-time help, this source should particularly be considered.

Unions. For a number of jobs, ranging from plumbers to publicists, the way to recruit qualified personnel is to go through their respective unions. In some instances, this is your only alternative.

Trade and professional associations. Most trade and professional associations are eager to assist employers in obtaining the services of their members. Whether you need help in finding an accountant, sales manager, management trainee, computer specialist, or supervisor, the local association is a good place to check.

As your business grows, other recruitment sources such as employee referrals, previous job applications on file, and industry contacts will become increasingly useful.

Utilize Application Forms

Job application forms simplify the hiring decision by helping you screen out unsuitable applicants and focus on qualified ones. The application can also serve as a starting point during an interview, suggesting questions or comments that make it easier to break the ice and establish a rapport with the applicant.

Your application form needn't be long or complicated to be effective. In fact, the simpler you can keep it, the better. The important thing is to cover the information that is relevant to a prospective employee's job performance.

APPLICATION FOR EMPLOYMENT

Application

Name_____ Date_____
       (Last)   (First)   (Middle)

Address_____ Telephone_____

Social security number_____ Are you over 18?_____

Have you ever been bonded?_____ Are you a U.S. citizen?_____

If not a citizen, do you have a work permit?_____ Number_____

May we contact your present and previous employers?_____

Employment History (Last position first)

	From	To	Name & Address	Position	Reason for leaving
1.					
2.					
3.					
4.					

Education

	Name & Address	From	To	Graduated
High School				
College				
Other				

References

	Name & Address	Telephone	Relationship
1.			
2.			

I understand that if I am employed and any statement is then found to be not true, I may be released immediately.

Signature_____ Date_____

In developing the job application form you will be using, keep in mind that federal law prohibits discriminating against anyone on the basis of race, sex, religion, color, or national origin. Nor can you automatically rule out an applicant because of age or because of a physical handicap. To stay in compliance with the law, your best bet is to restrict your questions to those that focus on an applicant's ability to do the work.

Conduct Interviews

Interviewing prospective employees gives you the opportunity to find out more about each applicant's employment background, skills, and education. Such additional factors as an applicant's enthusiasm, ability to communicate, poise, and personal appearance can also be evaluated.

In conducting interviews, you should select a private, comfortable location in which to talk. Trying to carry on a conversation over the sounds of machinery or ringing telephones is counterproductive. You want to put the applicant at ease so that you can gather the information you need. The trick is to get the other person talking. Too many interviewers dominate the conversation themselves, and then when it's time to make an evaluation they have little to go on.

The way to get the most out of interviews is to be ready for them. For a start, review the job application prior to each interview. This will give you some idea of the person you are about to meet. Keep the application with you during the interview as well, so that you can refer to it if needed or make notes on it. Many staffing experts also recommend writing out a few questions in advance. Then, instead of worrying about what to ask next, you can really listen to what's being said. Immediately after the interview is over, jot down your evaluation of the applicant before you forget anything.

Verify Information

Even if you're positive that you've found the best person for the job, don't hire anyone yet. Before you do, there's one more step: verify the information you've been given. Regardless of how favorable a first impression may be, there's no substitute for checking the facts. It's not a matter of doubting your own judgment; it's just good business sense.

In verifying academic information, ask to see an official copy of the applicant's record from each school attended. Dates of attendance, courses taken, and grades received should all appear on the record. To check an applicant's work history, contact previous employers. This can be done by phone or letter or in person. In so doing, though, be prepared to take all comments with a grain of salt; former employers sometimes exaggerate a past employee's attributes or failings. Your job is to try to separate the facts from the fiction.

The Hiring Decision Is Made

Congratulations! Having gone through the previous steps, with any luck you're now ready to select the person you want to hire. This is a time to celebrate—but not a time to rest on your laurels. The staffing process continues.

Provide Job Orientation

Each new employee needs to be made to feel comfortable in your business. Starting a new job is a cause for uncertainty, no matter how terrific the job is. Getting to know co-workers, keeping track of new duties and responsibilities, and attempting to figure out how the organization operates can easily overwhelm a new employee. It takes time to adjust to a new job. It also takes help from you.

The purpose of a job orientation program is to answer as many questions as possible about your business and the new employee's position within it. Right off the bat, the employee should be filled in on the company's policies and regulations as well as the employee's duties and responsibilities, compensation, and benefits.

Many businesses, small as well as large, provide new hires with an employee handbook that contains the information they need to know. While no substitute for personal communication exists, an employee handbook can help to put your business in the proper perspective and to simplify the employee's adjustment. In putting together a handbook, don't feel that it has to be a thick volume, complete with pictures and a fancy cover. A few typewritten pages of clearly presented information can generally do the job. Among the subjects you want to cover in detail are:

- The company's history.
- An explanation of the company's products or services.
- Company policies and procedures.
- Employee compensation benefits.

Provide Training

The welfare of both your business and your employees rests on the quality of training that you are able to provide. In order to carry out their current jobs and to obtain the skills necessary to advance into more challenging jobs, employees need guidance and training. Without it, skills and motivation begin to stagnate and decline, productivity drops off, and the business suffers. All needlessly.

A training program helps employees to grow so that they can help your business grow. Some of the kinds generally utilized are on-the-job training, job rotation, specialized training, and management development.

On-the-job training endeavors to instruct an employee in how to carry out a particular job assignment. Equally useful in training new employees and employees who are changing jobs, it consists of four parts:

1. *Preparation.* The trainer finds out what the employee already knows about the job.
2. *Demonstration.* The trainer shows the employee how to do the job.
3. *Application.* The employee does the job alone.
4. *Inspection.* The work is inspected and suggestions or comments made.

Job rotation allows employees to learn new jobs and broaden their skills by working at different assignments on a temporary basis. As a result, workers become more versatile, tedium is reduced, and scheduling is simplified because of worker flexibility.

Specialized training can enable an employee to hone old skills or master new ones. Through company-offered courses or outside courses at local colleges or trade schools, employees can learn how to operate a new piece of machinery, type faster, improve sales presentations, read a blueprint, or any number of things beneficial to both the employees and the company.

Management development is geared toward training people to enter management or to advance within the managerial ranks. By means of courses on such subjects as leadership, decision making, planning, and communication, employees can be groomed to accept more responsibility.

Evaluate Performance

Employees need a yardstick by which to measure their performance and progress. This can be supplied in the form of performance evaluation. Conducted at regular intervals, this evaluation should highlight an employee's strengths and pinpoint the areas that need improvement.

One method of evaluation that is popular with employees and employers alike is *management by objectives* (MBO). Its appeal stems from the fact that it contains no surprises or hidden clauses; everything expected of the employee is spelled out in advance as objectives. Furthermore, these objectives are decided upon jointly by the worker and the worker's boss. Together, as a team, they set down on paper the targets that the employee will strive to reach. Later, when it's time to evaluate the employee's performance, it's easy to see which objectives have been met and which ones need additional work. New objectives can then be set and the evaluation process continued.

Compensate Employees

In order to attract and retain high-caliber employees, it's necessary to compensate them at the going wage or better. Trying to get something for nothing just leads to employee dissatisfaction and high turnover. And if your employees feel that you're taking advantage of them, chances are that they'll find a way to take advantage of you. Work slowdowns and theft are just two of the many ways possible.

In addition to comparing favorably with the competition, your policy on wages should be an equitable one that rewards employees on the basis of merit. This instills loyalty and motivates employees to work harder and to expand their skills, so that they can increase their earnings.

Another kind of compensation that employees have come to expect is called *fringe benefits*. These consist of such components as a health plan, pension plan, life insurance, bonuses, and profit sharing. These vary from company to company and may not be applicable or affordable for your business. They should certainly be considered, however.

Monitor Employee Turnover

Once an employee quits, who cares what the employee thinks about your business? You do. It's just as important to pay heed to an employee's reason for leaving as it is to listen to a job applicant's reasons for wanting to work for you. This is your chance to find out something about your business that might help you to make it a better place in which to work. Hiring and training employees is costly and time-consuming. Any information associated with reducing turnover is worth listening to.

Before the employee leaves, an *exit interview* should be scheduled. During this interview, the employee should be asked the reasons for leaving (better salary, promotion, dissatisfaction with the job, return to school, spouse's job transfer). The employee's opinions regarding the company, its policies, and its personnel should also be solicited. Your goal here isn't to debate the issues or to convince a dissatisfied worker to stay, but to obtain information you can refer to in making future plans.

Staffing Checklist

In order to recruit, hire, and retain the best people available for your business, take a moment to answer the question in the Staffing Checklist on page 130.

Exit Interview Report

1. Name of employee	2. Date	3. Department	4. Shift	5. Date hired

6. Address	7. Male _____ Female _____	8. Marital status	9. Age	10. Education

11. Job title or position	12. Name of supervisor	13. Veteran?	14. Handicap?	15. Would you rehire?

16. Previous training

17. Type of separation

18. Reason(s) for separation

19. Indirect causes for separation

20. Action taken

STAFFING CHECKLIST

	Answer yes or no
1. Have you analyzed each job that you want filled?	_____
2. Have you prepared job descriptions?	_____
3. Do you know what sources to use in recruiting employees?	_____
4. Will you utilize an application form?	_____
5. Do you know the information that can and cannot be included on an application form?	_____
6. Do you know what to do to prepare for an interview?	_____
7. Will you verify the information received from each applicant that you are seriously considering?	_____
8. Have you decided on the kind of job orientation to give your new employees?	_____
9. Have you prepared an employee handbook?	_____
10. Do you know which form(s) of job training to utilize?	_____
11. Have you determined how often to evaluate your employees?	_____
12. Do you intend to use an evaluation form when evaluating employees?	_____
13. Will your employees be adequately compensated for the work they perform?	_____
14. Are you planning to monitor employee turnover?	_____
15. Will you use an exit interview report?	_____
16. Do you intend to listen to the advice of employees who are leaving and take advantage of worthwhile suggestions?	_____

Eleven

Developing Your Promotional Strategy

If you build a better mousetrap, the world may indeed beat a path to your door. But not without a little help from you. In the first place, before people can buy your mousetrap, they have to know about it. In the second place, they have to know where to find your door. In the third place, it helps if the people you're trying to reach are having trouble with rodents.

The U.S. Patent Office has issued patents by the thousand for inventions that never made it. Putting aside the problems of unworkable designs or excessive production cost, many of the inventions failed simply because of poor or nonexistent promotional strategies. Having created their better mousetraps, the inventors didn't know what to do with them.

Forming a business is much the same as inventing a new product. In order to succeed, each needs to be promoted. Having answered the questions at the beginning of Chapter 2 on determining the best location, you've already evaluated the need for your particular product or service. And you have a pretty good idea who your potential customers are. Knowing this much is half the battle. Now, what's left is to convert those potential customers into satisfied customers. That's where your promotional strategy comes in.

A promotional strategy is a game plan for reaching your target market—those people most likely to use your product or service. At the simplest, most direct level, your promotional strategy might consist of relying on a sign in front of your door and the word-of-mouth comments of your present customers. In some instances—if you're in a very small town, or if you offer unique products or services, or if you have a long-standing reputation, for example—this is sufficient. Normally, though, customers need more to go on before they are drawn to your business.

The goal of your promotional strategy should be to reach the greatest number of potential customers through the most economical use of your resources (money, personnel, and facilities). This entails tuning in to those channels of communication (by means of advertising and publicity) most widely used by your target customers. It also entails working within the limits of a budget to achieve the desired results.

Advertising

Advertising involves the purchasing of time or space in the various communications media for the purpose of promoting your business. The two categories of advertising are institutional and product. *Institutional advertising* promotes your business in general, emphasizing its good name and any contributions that it has made to the well-being of the community. *Product advertising* promotes the specific products or services you sell, emphasizing the benefits associated with buying them from you. An oil company, for instance, can emphasize the time and money it spends in exploring for new sources of fuel (institutional advertising), or it can emphasize the special additives that make its gasoline better than the rest (product advertising). Your own objectives will determine whether to use one or both of these approaches.

The Media

The advertising media generally favored are newspapers, magazines, radio, television, direct mail, yellow pages, and outdoor advertising. Other media include transit, specialty, movie theaters, flyers, church bulletins, and sponsoring sporting teams.

Each medium has its own unique characteristics and is capable of reaching large numbers of people. Depending on your message, target customers, budget, and lead time, some will be more suited to your needs than others.

First of all, is your *message* simple and direct ("You'll save more money at Jones's Hardware Store"), or is it more complicated, involving a detailed explanation (a listing of the nutrients in your special health food drink)? Does your message rely heavily on words, color, sound, or movement to make its point?

Second, is your *target customer* everyone (the mass market), or just a small segment of the market? The narrower your target, the greater the need to use selective media to reach it. Doctors, for instance, can be reached more effectively by means of a medical journal than a daytime soap opera.

Third, consider your *budget.* How much money can you spend? Despite the suitability of a particular medium, if you can't afford it there's no sense in building your promotional strategy around it.

Finally, what is your *lead time*? Do you want the advertisement to start this week, next month, next year? Lead times vary with the medium, and if you need a quick start, that limits your selection.

Newspapers

Newspapers, which have traditionally been the favorite means of advertising for retailers, currently account for almost a third of all advertising dollars spent in the United States.

Message. Newspapers are one of the best equipped of the media (along with magazines and direct mail) for explaining and describing a product. Not only is the space available, but the only limitation on time is the reader's attention span. The effectiveness of your message can be quickly and easily measured through the use of redeemable coupons in your ads and customer demand for the featured items. If no one brings in a coupon or asks for the product, the ad isn't working.

Target customer. Since newspapers are local, they reach the people in your own community. Their readers are your potential customers. For greater selectivity, your ad can be placed in the sections most likely to appeal to your target customer (sports, business, world news, entertainment, food, real estate). An ad for a restaurant might run in either the entertainment or the food section.

Budget. Newspaper rates are low compared to most other media. Even a business on a very limited budget can generally afford a small ad.

Lead time. Newspapers have the shortest lead time of the media. Some ads can be placed on as little as two or three days' notice. This gives you a great deal of flexibility in deciding when and what to advertise.

Limitations. Newspapers are short-lived; if your ad isn't read today, chances are that it won't ever be read. Reproduction quality is poor; products that require strong visual presentations are better served by other media. Most people don't read every page in a newspaper; unless careful attention is paid to your ad's placement, it could get lost in the shuffle.

Rates. Advertising space is sold in column inches (14 lines to an inch). An ad that's 2 columns wide by 3 inches deep occupies 6 column inches. The rate per column inch is based on a paper's circulation. The larger the circulation, the higher the rates.

Volume rates. Bigger advertisers are entitled to discounts. This means that the more space you buy, the lower the rate per column inch.

Preferred position rates. If you specify a particular position, page, or position on the page, the rate is higher. But if this gets people to see your ad, it's worth the money. Because of the way we read, ads at the upper right of the page generally have the most drawing power.

Classified rates. These rates are quoted by lines, rather than column inches. The ideal position is at the front of the classified section. The farther back that your ad appears, the larger the drop-off in readers.

Comparing costs. Depending on your location, there may be several newspapers to choose from. Based on each paper's rates and circulation, it's an easy matter to compare the costs and determine which is the best buy. This is done by measuring each papers cost per thousand people reached, or CPM.

$$\frac{\text{Cost of ad} \times 1,000}{\text{Total circulation}} = \text{CPM}$$

Newspaper A $$\frac{\$500 \times 1,000}{650,000} = 77\text{¢ per } 1,000$$

Newspaper B $$\frac{\$460 \times 1,000}{575,000} = 80\text{¢ per } 1,000$$

As you can see, although an ad in newspaper A is more expensive, its cost per thousand readers is actually less. This makes it the better buy.

Magazines

Though used primarily by large advertisers, magazines are now starting to grow in popularity with smaller advertisers as well. This is because of the increase in special-interest magazines. Unlike general-interest magazines, these focus on a single topic (films, needlepoint, travel, skiing, gardening) and enable advertisers to reach a specific audience.

Message. Like newspapers, magazines are well suited to conveying in-depth information, and their effectiveness can be readily measured. Reproduction values are high, so products that need color or strong visuals to make an impact look their best. Furthermore, people tend to read magazines at a more leisurely pace than newspapers and are inclined to save them afterward. This lengthens the lifespan of your ad.

Target customer. Magazines enable you to be as selective as you want in pinpointing your target customer. Through careful placement of your ads in the right special-interest magazines, you're virtually guaranteed of reaching a receptive audience.

Budget. Magazine ads can be expensive, particularly in national magazines with large circulations. But if you're willing to do some research, there are bargains to be found. For information about rates check the *Standard Rate and Data Service*, a monthly publication available at many libraries.

Lead Time. Magazines have a much longer lead time than newspapers. Ads normally must be received two or three months prior to publication.

Limitations. The long lead time reduces your flexibility; ads must be planned and space purchased well in advance. Magazine ads can get lost, too; positioning is important.

Rates. Space is usually sold by the page or fraction of a page. Some magazines also have classified or mail order sections in which space is sold by the line. These sections are generally at the back of the magazines. Rates are determined by circula-

137

tion. However, a magazine that caters to a particularly affluent or hard-to-reach audience may still be able to charge high rates despite a small circulation. Other determinants of rates are:

- *Color.* An ad that's in color is more expensive than a black-and-white ad.
- *Quantity discounts.* These are based on the amount of space purchased in a twelve-month period.
- *Frequency discounts.* These are based on the number of times space is purchased in a twelve-month period.
- *Positioning.* If a special position is requested there is an additional charge.

Comparing Costs. As with newspapers, magazines can be compared by the CPM technique to determine which is most economical.

Radio

Radio's main strength is its ability to reach people regardless of where they are or what they're doing. Whether at home, driving to work, or on vacation, people have their radios with them. In the United States today there are almost two radios per person, with 99 percent of all households having at least one radio.

Message. Radio uses words, music, and sound effects to communicate its message. It has strong emotional impact, which is derived from its ability to establish a rapport with the audience and move listeners to action. Jingles and slogans are common in radio commercials because listeners remember them later. This helps to reinforce brand identification.

Target customer. Radio stations, like special-interest magazines, gear themselves toward a particular audience. Through the program format you select (top 40 rock music, country music, classical music, middle of the road, easy listening, talk show, news) it's possible to zero in on your target customer.

Budget. The cost of purchasing air time depends on a program's popularity and the frequency of your commercials. To determine costs, check the Standard Rate and Data Service.

Lead time. Lead times vary. Certain programs may be booked as much as a year in advance, while others have immediate openings.

Limitations. Many radio stations are competing for audiences; this may make it necessary to buy time on a number of stations to reach all your target customers. To be effective at all, your commercial needs to be broadcast more than once; this repetition increases your costs. The lifespan of your commercial is just seconds; unlike a print advertisement, it gets only one chance to communicate your message. Radio is a medium without visuals; if your product has to be seen to be believed you're wasting your money.

Rates. Time is sold in units of 60 seconds or less—that is, in 10, 15, 30, and 60 second spots. Although 60 second commercials were the most used prior to the 1970s, the trend is now toward shorter ones, with 30 second spots currently the most popular.

Rates are based on both a station's coverage and its circulation. *Coverage* is the geographical area covered by the station's signal. *Circulation* refers to the potential number of listeners in the area. Since the number of listeners can vary throughout the day, different rates are charged for different time periods.

Drive time. This is the most expensive time of day because it covers the intervals from 6 to 10 A.M. and from 4 to 7 P.M., when people are in their cars driving to and from work.

Run-of-the-station (ROS). This is the cheapest time because it allows the station to put your commercial anywhere it pleases.

Weekly plan. A weekly plan offers a lower rate to advertisers purchasing a package of time. Each package contains a variety of time slots, ranging from drive time to ROS.

Comparing costs. Stations can be compared by means of the cost-per-thousand technique.

Television

Though television trails newspapers as the most picked advertising medium, it is rapidly closing in on the top spot. The reason for television's growing popularity is simple: numbers. Currently 97% of all American households have one or more television sets, and the average family watches for more than six hours per day. The newest of the media, television's impact on its audience is still being explored. But the fact that it can shape attitudes and change opinions is already known.

Message. Television is the most intimate of the media; combining sight, sound, color, and motion, it takes your presentation right into the viewer's home. Television lets you show off your product, rather than just tell about it. The viewer sees it in a natural setting that encourages acceptance. (If the people in the commercial are satisfied with the product, why shouldn't the viewer be too?)

Target customer. More than any of the other media, television is a mass medium. At any one time, millions of viewers are watching. Programs like the Super Bowl, the World Series, and the Miss America Pageant may be tuned in by more than 50 million viewers. The question is: Are these your target customers? In selecting a program on which to advertise, it's as important to check the data describing the viewers (age, sex, income, interests) as it is to check the number of people who are watching.

Budget. Unfortunately, advertising on television is expensive. Regardless of its appeal, the majority of small businesses will find it beyond their budgets. However, local and cable television stations offer considerably reduced rates, and these may be a viable alternative. For further information, check the Standard Rate and Data Service.

Lead time. Top rated television shows are likely to be booked a year in advance. Time slots on less popular shows and new shows are generally available on a few days' notice.

Limitations. Television has less selectivity than the other media; using it to reach a small target audience could be an exercise in overkill. Viewers often leave the room during commercials; getting and holding their attention isn't easy. Television commercials, like radio commercials, become more effective with repetition; this adds to your cost.

Rates. Time is sold in units of 60 seconds or less, with 30 second spots currently the most favored. Rates vary on the basis of the time period selected and the size of the audience for a given program—hence the importance of the Nielsen and Arbitron ratings, which rank programs in the order of their popularity.

Prime time. This is the most costly time. It covers the hours from 7 to 11 P.M., when the greatest number of viewers are watching television.

Discounts. These are available on essentially the same terms as those offered by radio stations.

Comparing costs. The CPM technique applies.

Direct Mail

Direct mail refers to any printed material of a promotional nature, that is mailed directly to the intended customer—brochures, letters, price lists, catalogs, coupons. This is currently the third most popular choice with advertisers and is used by the majority of businesses, large and small.

Message. Like newspapers and magazines, direct mail is one of the best formats for conveying in-depth information. It also offers the greatest flexibility, since any message can be sent to anyone at any time. Direct mail is regularly used to:

- Inform customers of sales.
- Introduce new products.

- Announce price changes.
- Solicit mail order business.
- Solicit phone order business.
- Maintain customer contact.
- Reach new customers.
- Develop your image.

Target customer. The success of a direct mail campaign is primarily determined by the mailing list. Unless your mailing is going out to the people who are likely to buy your product, you're wasting both time and money. How can you obtain a mailing list that's right for you? You can either purchase it from someone else or build your own list. There are a number of companies in the business of compiling and selling mailing lists. These lists are available in literally thousands of categories (women between the ages of 18 and 45, teenagers, skiers, photography enthusiasts, recent graduates, cooking enthusiasts). Regardless of your target market, there is probably an applicable list. The cost may be as low as $6 per thousand names or as high as $100 per thousand.

If you prefer to build your own list, some of the sources you may be able to use are:

- Your own customers.
- Telephone directories.
- Professional, trade, and industrial directories.
- Credit bureaus.
- Newspaper announcements (wedding, graduation, birth, new business).
- Construction permits on file in municipal and county offices.

Budget. Direct mail's flexibility makes it possible to structure a campaign to meet practically any budget. You should consider:

- The cost of the mailing list.
- The cost of the package (printed materials).
- The cost of postage.

- The cost of labor (addressing, stuffing, and sealing envelopes).

The more extensive the mailing, the higher the cost.

Lead Time. You control the lead time.

Limitations. In terms of unit costs, direct mail is expensive; it has the highest cost-per-thousand of the media. There's only a fine line between direct mail and junk mail; make sure you are sending your mailing to the people who really want it.

Rates. Since there is no space or time to be purchased, there are no set rates to consider.

Yellow Pages

Any business that has a telephone is entitled to a one-line listing, free of charge, in the yellow pages of the telephone book. Many businesses choose to increase their visibility by purchasing display ads as well.

Message. A yellow pages display ad is an attention getting device. Since your ad is surrounded by those of your competition, it's important that you focus in on the best way to differentiate yourself from the rest—lowest prices, widest selection, friendly service, or whatever.

Target customer. The main advantage of yellow pages advertising is its ability to reach your target customers at the time they want to buy. Thus your audience is presold. Having already decided *what* to buy, customers are just looking for the right *place* to buy it.

Budget. Yellow pages ads are inexpensive in comparison to the other media.

Lead time. Your ad must be placed before the closing date for inclusion in the current directory.

Limitations. You can't make changes in your ad; it runs as is until the next directory printing.

Rates. Rates vary from directory to directory, based on the size of the territory covered. Contact the yellow pages sales representative in your area for full information.

Outdoor Advertising

Outdoor advertising involves the use of signs, posters, and billboards to promote your business. In the simplest sense, they can serve as a marker identifying your location. In the broadest sense, they can create an image—getting people to think of your name whenever they think of a particular product.

Message. Your message needs to be simple and direct. Concise copy, bold graphics, and a recognizable product are essential. Remember, the average passerby spends less than ten seconds reading your ad.

Target customer. Although outdoor advertising is visible to anyone who cares to look, a fairly high degree of selectivity can be achieved through the geographic placement of your advertisement. For instance, ads for airlines, hotels, restaurants, shops, and tourist attractions are typically found on billboards near airports and along freeways where travelers can see them.

Budget. The costs of outdoor advertising are among the lowest of the media.

Lead time. If you're just using signs at your place of business, the only lead time is the production and installation time. In the case of posters and billboards, space is rented on an availability basis and there may be a waiting list for the locations you want.

Limitations. Your advertisement is competing with numerous others; its effectiveness hinges on its ability to command attention. Some people regard outdoor advertising as a form of visual pollution; part of the response to your ads may thus be negative.

Rates. The rates charged for posters and billboards are based on the size and location of the space being leased. Locations are classified by territories, which are priced according to traffic counts. The higher the count, the higher the cost.

Comparing costs. The CPM technique can be used to compare territories to determine the most economical purchase.

Other Advertising Media

Some of the other forms of advertising you may wish to consider are transit advertising (messages are displayed on the exteriors and interiors of trains, buses, and taxicabs); specialty advertising (your company's name or logo is imprinted on such items as calendars, memo pads, book markers, ashtrays, matches, key chains, and T-shirts); flyers (these can be handed out to passers-by or placed on automobile windshields); and theater screen advertising (ads are shown during intermissions).

Publicity

In addition to advertising, you can use publicity to promote your business. This involves getting information about your company's activities or products reported in the news media. Such coverage is provided when the information is thought to have news value or to be of interest to the public.

Although publicity and advertising are similar, they differ in three vital areas: cost, control, and credibility. Publicity is free. There is no cost to you for the media coverage you receive. Nor do you have any control over that coverage. Unlike advertising, publicity can be favorable or unfavorable—as likely to point out your business's flaws as its accomplishments. If a news broadcast chooses to focus on a lawsuit that's been brought against you, rather than on your volunteer service to the community, there's nothing you can do about it. This very lack of control is what gives publicity its greatest strength—credibility. The fact that it's the news media, rather than a sponsor, delivering your message makes it more believable than advertising.

While it's impossible to control the publicity you get, it *is* possible to influence it. The way to do this is by maintaining good press relations: providing timely and accurate information in the form of press releases pointing out the angle that makes your story interesting or newsworthy, being available to answer questions, and not making unreasonable demands. By learning to work within the limitations of publicity, you can put yourself in a position to take full advantage of it.

Preparing an Advertising Budget

In preparing their advertising budgets, the majority of businesses base their allocations on a percentage of annual past sales, estimated sales, or a combination of these. For example, 2 percent of $100,000 in sales equals an advertising budget of $2,000. Some of the reasons for this method's general acceptance are that it gives you more to go on than guesswork, it emphasizes the relationship between advertising and sales, and it's easy to use.

In determining the percent of sales you want to invest in advertising, you should consider your business's needs, the competition, and the economic environment. To find out what similar businesses are spending, it's a good idea to check such sources as trade journals and the reports published by Dun & Bradstreet, Robert Morris Associates, the Accounting Corporation of America, Census Bureau, and Internal Revenue Service.

Once you have calculated your budget, the next step is to allocate it over the coming year, indicating the amount to be spent each month and the media to receive it. Keep in mind that some months will require greater expenditures than others. Also, don't forget to plan for any sales or special events you wish to promote.

SAMPLE ADVERTISING BUDGET

Camera Shop

Sales for 19XX	$100,000
Ad budget as percent of sales	4%
Total ad budget	$ 4,000

Direct mail (10,000 pieces at 18¢ each)	$1,800
Handouts (8,000 pieces at 5¢ each)	400
Yellow pages (12 months)	480
Newspapers (12 cooperative ads with manufacturers' assistance)	1,320
Total ad budget	$4,000

Best selling days
  Christmas
  Graduation
  Summer

	Direct mail	Handouts	Yellow Pages	News- papers	Total
January	$ 450		$ 40	$ 110	$ 600
February			40	110	150
March			40	110	150
April			40	110	150
May	450		40	110	600
June		$200	40	110	350
July	450		40	110	600
August			40	110	150
September			40	110	150
October			40	110	150
November	450		40	110	150
December		200	40	110	350
Total	$1,800	$400	$480	$1,320	$4,000

ADVERTISING FOR SMALL BUSINESSES

Business category	Typical ad budget as percent of sales	Media selected
Apparel stores	2.5–3.5	Direct mail, newspapers, radio
Auto supply shops	1.0–2.0	Direct mail, fliers, newspapers, yellow pages
Bars and grills	1.0–1.5	Magazines, newspapers, yellow pages
Beauty salons	2.5–4.0	Direct mail, newspapers, yellow pages
Book stores	1.8–2.2	Newspapers, yellow pages
Cafeterias	2.0–2.6	Newspapers, radio, yellow pages
Catering services	2.0–3.0	Direct mail, fliers, yellow pages
Dry cleaners	1.2–1.7	Direct mail, fliers, newspapers, yellow pages
Fabric stores	1.0–2.5	Newspapers, yellow pages
Flower shops	1.0–2.0	Newspapers, radio, yellow pages
Gift shops	2.0–2.5	Magazines, newspapers, radio, yellow pages
Graphic arts specialists	0.5–1.5	Direct mail, magazines, newspapers, yellow pages
Health clubs	3.0–5.0	Direct mail, newspapers, radio, television, yellow pages
Ice cream parlors	1.0–2.5	Newspapers, radio, yellow pages
Jewelry stores	2.5–3.5	Direct mail, magazines, radio, television, yellow pages
Locksmiths	0.5–1.5	Direct mail, transit, yellow pages
Mail order	18.0–30.0	Direct mail, magazines, newspapers, television

Photography stores	2.5–4.0	Direct mail, magazines, newspapers, radio, yellow pages
Sporting goods stores	2.0–2.5	Newspapers, radio, television, yellow pages
Stationery stores	2.0–3.0	Newspapers, yellow pages
Ticket agencies	3.0–5.0	Magazines, newspapers, radio, yellow pages
TV and appliance stores	1.5–2.5	Newspapers, radio, television, yellow pages
Upholsterers	0.2–0.8	Shopping guides, yellow pages
Wedding consultants	1.5–2.5	Direct mail, magazines, yellow pages

Promotional Strategy Checklist

To help launch your promotional campaign and reach your target market in the most economical way possible, answer the questions in the Promotional Strategy checklist on p. 149.

PROMOTIONAL STRATEGY CHECKLIST

	Answer yes or no
1. Do you know who your potential customers are?	_____
2. Have you established a game plan for reaching your target market?	_____
3. Do you know the difference between institutional and product advertising?	_____
4. Do you know the benefits and limitations of each of the following media?	
Newspaper	_____
Magazines	_____
Radio	_____
Television	_____
Direct mail	_____
Yellow pages	_____
Outdoor advertising	_____
5. Can you compare costs between like forms of advertising (CPM)?	_____
6. Do you know the rates of the different media?	_____
7. Do you know the difference between advertising and publicity?	_____
8. Do you know how to maintain good press relations?	_____
9. Have you prepared an advertising budget?	_____
10. Have you determined which are the best advertising media for your business?	_____
11. Do you know what media are being used by the competition?	_____
12. Do you keep track of competitors' advertising campaigns?	_____
13. Do you know the best times to advertise during the year?	_____

Twelve

Safeguarding
Your Business

The very act of forming your own business entails risk. The rewards of prosperity and self-fulfillment must be balanced against the risks of financial loss and personal dissatisfaction. There are no sure things in business. Still, such factors as planning, experience, adequate financing, managerial expertise, creativity, and a willingness to work hard can swing the odds in your favor. For these to be effective, though, you need an ongoing program of risk management.

Suppose any of the following should happen:

- Your building is damaged by fire.
- A customer is hurt in your store.
- An employee steals merchandise.
- A car drives through your store window.
- Your accountant embezzles a large sum of money.
- An employee is injured on the job.
- Your store is burglarized.
- Your business is suffering because of shoplifting.
- A partner dies.

What would you do? A likely answer is, "call my insurance agent." But relying on insurance is only one of the ways to deal with these hazards.

Risk Management

An effective program of risk management enables you to cope with risks by eliminating them, reducing them, accepting them, or transferring them. These methods can be used singly or in combination, depending on the risk as well as on your own circumstances.

Eliminating the risk. Certain risks can be entirely eliminated. Among these are the risk of employee injury because of substandard materials or unsafe equipment, the risk of customer injury because of a hazardous store layout, and the risk of fire because of faulty wiring. There's no excuse for allowing risks that are solely the result of negligence or indifference. One who persists in doing so could wind up not only financially liable but criminally liable as well. And it's not enough merely to carry insurance. Gross negligence, or the flagrant violation of health and safety standards, is sufficient ground for an insurance carrier to void your policy.

Reducing the risks. It would be impossible for you to eliminate every business risk, even if you were aware of every one. Your best bet, then, is to reduce the risks. Close evaluation of your workplace, workers, and customers will enable you to take precautionary actions so as to reduce most of your business risks.

The risk of falling off a ladder can't be eliminated; but the use of safety ladders, with guard rails on either side, can reduce the risk. Keeping all merchandise boxes, cleaning supplies, tools, and electrical cords clear of customer walkways reduces the risk of having customers trip and injure themselves. The risks of breakage and theft can be reduced by displaying merchandise in locked cases. Electronic tags on merchandise, alert salespeople, closed circuit cameras, burglar alarms, and security guards can also help you to combat theft.

Accepting the risk. Self-insurance, a method whereby you create your own contingency fund to pay for whatever business losses might arise, is another way of coping with risk. This enables a business to protect itself while at the same time avoiding payment of insurance premiums. Unfortunately, the protection this method provides is usually inadequate. Given current high replacement costs for buildings, equipment, furniture, and fixtures, as well as the staggering amounts of some judgment claims in liability cases, a small business that relies solely on self-insurance could easily be wiped out.

A policy of accepting the risk might be applied, however, when the risk cannot be eliminated and buying outside insurance is not profitable. For instance, if your losses from shoplifting are less than the insurance premiums to protect yourself against it, accepting the losses makes more sense. Furthermore, even when you do carry insurance against a particular type of risk, part of the risk usually must be accepted because of the policy's deductible provision.

Transferring the risk. The purchase of coverage from an insurance company enables businesses to transfer their risks. In exchange for a fee, the insurance company accepts the risks that the business wishes to be protected against. In effect, when you buy insurance you arrange to absorb small periodic losses (premiums) rather than a large uncertain loss. If your property is to be adequately protected and large damage claims that result from public liability or employee injury suits are to be avoided, insurance is a necessity.

Types of Insurance Coverage

Fire insurance. In a standard fire insurance policy your building, the property contained within it, and property temporarily removed from it because of fire are protected against damage inflicted by fire or lightning. This coverage does not extend to accounting records, bills, deeds, money, securities, or manuscripts. Nor are you protected against such hazards as windstorms, hail, smoke, explosions, vandalism, automatic sprinkler leakage, and malicious mischief. To guard excluded valuables and protect yourself against loss from these hazards, you must obtain additional coverage. Neither fire resulting from war nor actions taken under the orders of a civil authority are covered by insurance.

Depending on the terms of your policy, compensation may be made in any of three ways: (1) the insurance carrier may pay you the current cash value of the damaged property, (2) the property may be repaired or replaced, or (3) the property may be taken over by the insurer, who then reimburses you at its appraised value.

Most fire insurance policies are written for a three-year period, and both you and the insurer have the right to cancel. You may cancel your policy at any time. The insurer, however, must give you five days' notice before canceling. In either event, you will be reimbursed for any premiums that have been paid in advance. But if you are the one to cancel, a penalty as set forth in your policy may be assessed against your refund.

In order to keep your fire insurance policy valid, it's your responsibility to use all reasonable means to protect the insured property both before and after a fire. If you knowingly increase the fire hazard—by renting part of your building to a fireworks manufacturer, for example—this could void your policy. Hiding pertinent information from the insurer, or leaving your building unoccupied for more than 60 days, is also cause for voiding your policy.

Should it become necessary for you to file an insurance claim, you will be required to provide the insurance company with a complete inventory list, detailing the types, quantities, and values of the damaged property. Unless an extension is granted, you generally have sixty days in which to do this.

Liability insurance. As the operator of your own business, you are responsible for the safety of your employees and customers. If a customer slips on a wet floor, you may be liable for damages. You're also responsible for the products or services you sell. For instance, the owner of a garage could be held liable for using a car wax that strips the paint off a customer's car, or if a mechanic forgets to set the hand brake on a car and it rolls into the street and causes an accident. In the first case, the garage owner might have to cover the cost of a new paint job. In the second, there's no telling how much the cost might be. Was the car damaged? Were other cars damaged? Was anyone injured in the accident? These are just the physical damages for which the garage owner may be liable. What about the mental anguish of the parties involved in the accident? By the time all the costs have been added in, the entire assets of the garage could be wiped out.

Most liability policies cover losses stemming from bodily injury or property damage claims, expenses for medical services required at the time of the accident, investigation, and court costs.

The actual amount that your policy will pay depends on both the limit per accident and the limit per person provided for in it. For example, if your policy has a per-accident limit of $400,000 and a per-person limit of $100,000, and if one person receives a $300,000 judgment against you, the insurance company will pay only $100,000. This means you are responsible for paying the remaining $200,000 even though it is within your per-accident limit. The guide word here is *caution.* Make sure you understand and agree with any limitations in your policy. If the limit is $100,000 per person, is that adequate coverage?

If an accident does occur, even if it seems minor, contact your insurance agent immediately. This enables the insurance company to begin its investigation while the relevent information is readily available. Failure to notify the company can void your policy.

Automobile insurance. If you plan to use one or more cars or trucks in your business, automobile insurance is a must. Coverage can be provided to protect you against:

- Bodily injury claims.
- Property damage claims.
- Medical payments.
- Uninsured motorist damages.
- Damage to your vehicles.
- Towing costs.

The amount of coverage you need and the costs of an automobile insurance policy depend on the number of cars or trucks being insured; their value; the kinds of driving that will be done (making deliveries, hauling equipment, driving clients around); and your location. When five or more motor vehicles are used in your business, you can generally insure them under a low-cost fleet policy. As far as deductibles go, the higher they are, the lower your premiums.

You may find that automobile insurance is a good buy even if you don't plan to use any motor vehicles in your business. This is because you could be held liable for employees or subcontractors who operate their own vehicles, or those of customers, while on company business.

Workers' compensation insurance. Common law requires that an employer (1) provide employees with a safe place to work, (2) hire competent co-workers, (3) provide safe tools, and (4) warn employees of existing danger. An employer who fails to do so is liable for damages, including claims for on-the-job injury and occupational diseases. Sometimes payments can be required for the remainder of the disabled worker's life.

Under workers' compensation insurance, the insurer pays all sums you are legally required to pay a claimant. One way to save money on this insurance is to make sure your employees are properly classified. Since rates vary with the degree of hazard associated with each occupational category, improperly classifying an employee in a high-risk occupation raises your rates. Another way to save money is to use safety measures that will lower your accident rate and thereby reduce premiums.

Business interruption insurance. Many business owners fail to purchase business interruption insurance because they don't think they need it. If a building burns down, they think a standard fire insurance policy will suffice. But what about the loss of business income during the months it takes to rebuild? What about the expenses that continue to mount up even though your doors are closed—taxes, interest on loans, salaries, rent, utilities? Yet not until it is too late does many a business owner realize that fire insurance alone isn't enough.

Only business interruption insurance covers your fixed expenses and expected profits during the time your business is closed down. And make sure that the policy is written to provide coverage in the event that your business isn't totally shut down, but is seriously disrupted. Some policies pay off only in the event of a total shutdown. You should also remember that an indirect peril could force you to suspend operations as well. What if an important supplier's or customer's plant burned down, temporarily interrupting your business? What if your power, water, or phone service were disrupted for a spell? Protection against these hazards can be written into your business interruption policy, but you have to ask for it.

Glass insurance. Although it may seem insignificant, glass insurance is something most business should have. The costs of replacing broken plate glass windows, panels, doors, signs, and display cases are so high that you can't afford to be without it. Furthermore, delays in making the replacement can result in vandalism or theft, which in turn results in additional property loss.

A glass insurance policy covers the cost not only of replacing the glass itself, but of redoing any letter or ornamentation on the glass, installing the glass (including temporary glass or boards, if needed), and repairing any frame damage. The only exclusions in the standard all-risk glass insurance policy are for glass damage from fire or war. And, in the case of fire, your fire insurance policy provides coverage.

Fidelity bonds. Most new business owners are unaware that, on the average, thefts by employees far surpass business losses from burglary, robbery, and shoplifting. The accountant who embezzles thousands of dollars and then goes to Acapulco and the salesclerk who dips into the cash drawer come readily to mind. Less obvious examples include putting fictitious employees on the payroll and pocketing their paychecks; ringing up lower prices on merchandise sold to friends or accomplices; stealing merchandise, equipment, or supplies; misappropriating company property for personal use; lying on expense vouchers; and falsifying time cards.

Unless you or members of your immediate family handle all phases of your business operation, you should obtain fidelity bond protection. This is available in three formats: individual bonds, schedule bonds, and blanket bonds. *Individual bonds* cover theft by a specific named individual. *Schedule bonds* list every name or position to be covered. *Blanket bonds,* the most encompassing of the three, cover all employees without reference to individual names or positions.

Before an employee is bonded, the insurance company issuing the bond conducts a character investigation to determine whether anything is known of past acts of dishonesty. Then, if the employee is deemed bondable, coverage is provided. If a prospective employee refuses to be bonded, this could be a tip-off that the applicant has something to hide.

Crime insurance. Crime insurance covers you against business losses resulting from the criminal activities of people who aren't associated with your business. The three categories of crime insurance are burglary insurance, robbery insurance, and comprehensive insurance.

1. *Burglary insurance* protects your safes and inventory against thefts in which there is evidence of forcible entry. This means that, if a thief enters through an unlocked door or window without disturbing the premises, your burglary policy does not cover any losses. Nor does the standard burglary policy protect accounting records, manuscripts, or certain valuables, such as furs, which are kept in display windows. To cover these, additional insurance is necessary. Besides protecting you against losses from stolen property, burglary insurance provides coverage for damage sustained during the burglary.

2. *Robbery* differs from burglary in that it involves a face-to-face confrontation. The robber actually uses force, or the threat of violence, to take property from the person guarding it. A *robbery insurance* policy covers the money, property, or securities taken, as well as property damage that occurs during the robbery. Another feature of this policy is that it isn't limited to robberies that take place inside your building. Thus if you are robbed while making a delivery you are covered.

3. *Comprehensive insurance* is popular because, in addition to protecting you against burglary and robbery, it also protects against a variety of other hazards, including counterfeit money and forged checks. For instance, deception does not constitute robbery. If a con artist tricks you or an employee into parting with property, no force or threat of violence is involved. Therefore, it isn't a robbery, and unless you have a comprehensive policy you aren't covered. Coverage is also provided against the thief who gains entry to your business without any apparent use of force.

Personal insurance. Just as there's a need to insure your property against loss, there's an equal need to insure both yourself and your employees. Group health and life insurance, a retirement plan, and key personnel insurance all help to do this. The need for these may seem a long way off, but more and more small businesses are offering an employee benefits package that includes health and life insurance as a way of retaining valued personnel. If you decide to incorporate a retirement plan too, there's another advantage. Contributions made to the plan for yourself and employees are deductible from your federal income tax.

Key personnel insurance, long a staple in the insurance portfolio of major corporations, can be just as necessary for the small business owner. Could your business survive the death or disability of a partner or a key employee? If not, key personnel insurance can at least ease the loss. The proceeds from the insurance are exempt from income tax and payable directly to the business. The policy itself has a cash value and may be used as loan collateral.

Recognizing Warning Signals

The old adage that an ounce of prevention is worth a pound of cure readily pertains to risk management. But before you can take precautionary measures to head off an impending danger, you have to recognize the danger. The way to do this is to be alert to the warning signals around you. The following examples indicate a fire, accident, or theft waiting to happen . . . if it hasn't already:

Fire
1. Overloaded circuits.
2. Fuse blowouts.
3. Frayed electrical cords.
4. Overheating of equipment.
5. Fire extinguishers inoperative or inaccessible.
6. Trash piled up.
7. Smoking permitted in high-risk areas.
8. Improper procedures in use, storage, or disposal of flammable materials.
9. Power plant, heating, ventilation, and air conditioning equipment not checked at regular intervals.

Accident
1. Workers inadequately trained for their jobs.
2. Lack of safety rules or failure to enforce them.
3. Use of substandard materials or equipment.
4. Poor quality control.
5. A hazardous layout.
6. Admitting customers to the work area.
7. Letting customers use equipment themselves.
8. Lack of knowledge about products you sell.

Employee theft
1. Inadequate employee reference checks.
2. An employee who refuses to take an annual vacation.
3. An employee who never leaves the work area during lunch.
4. An employee who always arrives at work early and stays late.
5. One employee handling all bookkeeping procedures.
6. Expenses that are higher than predicted.
7. Inventory shortages.
8. Finding merchandise or equipment in trash bins.
9. Checks and money orders left sitting on desktops.
10. Unfamiliar names on the payroll.
11. An increase in sales returns.
12. Slow collections.

On the surface, none of these examples is proof of embezzlement, but their occurrence does indicate the need for additional investigation or tightened management controls.

Crime
1. Accepting checks without asking to see proper identification.
2. Accepting checks that have been endorsed twice.
3. Accepting blank checks that don't have computer-coded characteristics.
4. Keeping large amounts of money in cash registers.
5. Inattention to customers when they—

     a. Wear loose clothing.

     b. Carry a large purse or open shopping bag.

     c. Seem nervous or anxious.

     d. Wander into a restricted area.

     e. Are left unsupervised in dressing rooms.

6. Easily removable tickets on merchandise.
7. Failure at the cash register to open and inspect items that might conceal stolen goods.
8. Messy displays that make it difficult to spot what's there and what's missing.
9. Employee unfamiliarity with the merchandise your store carries.
10. Poor lighting.
11. Unsuitable locks on doors and windows.
12. Loose handling of keys.

Insurance Checklist

To make sure that you've adequately insured your business, use the Insurance Checklist to indicate the coverage you need.

INSURANCE CHECKLIST

Type of insurance	Purchase	Do not purchase
Property insurance		
Fire	_____	_____
Windstorm	_____	_____
Hail	_____	_____
Smoke	_____	_____
Explosion	_____	_____
Vandalism	_____	_____
Water damage	_____	_____
Glass	_____	_____
Liability insurance	_____	_____
Workers' compensation	_____	_____
Business interruption	_____	_____
Dishonesty		
Fidelity	_____	_____
Robbery	_____	_____
Burglary	_____	_____
Comprehensive	_____	_____
Personal		
Health	_____	_____
Life	_____	_____
Key personnel	_____	_____

Thirteen

Franchising

An alternative to forming your own business from scratch is to purchase a franchise. According to Department of Commerce statistics, franchising has grown to such proportions that half a million franchised operations now account for annual sales totaling $300 billion—more than 30 percent of all U.S. retail sales. Although commonly associated with fast food outlets, franchising's application is not limited to the food service industry. Franchises have become particularly visible in a variety of areas, including hotels and motels, print shops, automobile dealerships, service stations, beauty salons, dance studios, music stores, employment agencies, accounting services, and real estate brokerages. In fact, there seem to be few, if indeed any, businesses that don't lend themselves to franchising. The most recent entrants have been the legal and medical professions.

The boom in franchising began shortly after World War II and has continued ever since, despite fluctuations in the economy and added government regulations. Franchising's boosters predict that the 1980s will be even better since franchising offers investors job security and a hedge against inflation. Franchising's critics, on the other hand, are quick to point out that many who enter into franchising agreements end up working harder and earning less than they expected.

The Definition of Franchising

Franchising is a method of doing business whereby a company (the franchisor) grants to others (the franchisees) the rights to sell, distribute, or market the company's products or services. In so doing, franchisees are permitted to use the franchisor's name, trademarks, reputation, and selling techniques. To obtain these rights, each franchisee agrees to pay the franchisor a sum of money (the franchise fee), or a percentage of annual gross sales, or both. Many franchisees agree to purchase equipment or supplies from the franchisor as well.

Franchisors view franchising as a way to expand their businesses without having to rely on loans or stock issues for the necessary capital. In addition to providing expansion capital, franchisees generally can be counted on to bring high levels of energy and commitment to the company—a real plus, particularly if the going gets rough. Franchisees, for their part, view franchising as a way to tap into a good thing—a sort of hitch-your-wagon-to-a-going-concern strategy.

The Price

How much does it cost to purchase a franchise? That depends. Your initial investment can vary from a few thousand dollars to upward of a quarter of a million. On top of that is the annual percentage of gross sales, or royalty fee, required by most franchisors. This can be as high as 18 percent. Other charges may also be stipulated in the franchise agreement. Franchising, albeit an alternative to forming your own business from scratch, is not necessarily a cheap alternative.

Franchising's Advantages and Disadvantages

In order to determine whether the franchising route is right for you, take a look at both the advantages and disadvantages of buying a franchise.

The Advantages

Only limited experience is needed. As a franchisee you have access to the franchisor's experience. Instead of spending years learning the ropes in your intended business, you can be running it.

Training and continued assistance are provided. Rather than being left to sink or swim on your own, you have the franchisor there to provide additional support. This includes training programs and the ongoing services of consultants.

Financing is often available. The franchisor may permit you to make partial payment of your start-up costs (construction, equipment, inventory, promotion, and so on) and defer the balance over a period of years. This reduces the amount of capital immediately needed for your initial investment.

Purchasing power can be increased. It's often possible to purchase the products, supplies, equipment, and services used in your business directly from the franchisor at reduced rates. This enables you to stretch your dollars farther.

Promotion is generally strong. Franchisors put a great deal of effort into making their companies' names recognizable to the public. As a result of the franchisor's promotional campaign, your business benefits.

Customer acceptance is high. Since the goods and services of the franchisor are proven and well known, your business has virtually instant pulling power. Whereas a new business might spend years developing its reputation, yours is already established.

The Disadvantages

Guidelines must be followed. The franchisor sets the rules; your freedom to make decisions is limited by the necessity to follow standardized procedures and offer specific products or services.

Contracts tend to favor the franchisor. Since the franchise agreement is prepared by the franchisor, your bargaining power may be less than equal. Should a dispute arise, the franchisor generally has the edge.

Profits are shared with the franchisor. Normally franchisees are required to pay the franchisor a percentage of annual gross sales, thus reducing their own profits. In the event that your business fails to make a profit, this percentage must still be paid.

Transfer of ownership is limited. Your right to dispose of your franchise is restricted by the provisions of the franchise agreement. This means you may not be permitted to sell it to the highest bidder, bequeath it to a relative or friend in your will, or even give it away without the franchisor's approval.

Purchasing power can be reduced. Some franchisees have been required to purchase the products, supplies, equipment, and services used in their businesses only from the franchisor, even when other sources could provide them for less. The courts now consider such tie-in practices to be illegal, and you should be wary of any agreement that imposes them.

Other franchisees' actions reflect on you. A consumer who receives poor services in another one of the franchisor's outlets is likely to assume your franchise offers poor service too. Your business suffers as a result, regardless of its merits.

Paperwork is time-consuming. The franchisor requires that you fill out a variety of reports, which takes time. Unless you're organized, you could end up buried under an avalanche of paperwork.

The Franchise Agreement

The franchise agreement forms the basis for your relationship with the franchisor. Therefore, it must state clearly and in adequate detail the rights and responsibilities of both parties to the agreement. Anything that's ambiguous should be clarified at the outset. Waiting until later to straighten it out can have unfortunate consequences. And make sure that you are willing to accept *all* of the provisions contained in the contract. Once you've signed the agreement, you will be bound by it. If you find a clause unreasonable, try to have it deleted from the contract or modified. Barring these possibilities, you may decide not to enter into an agreement with the franchisor. The best way to protect yourself is to obtain the advice of an attorney before signing any papers.

In evaluating the merits of a particular franchise agreement, you should give careful attention to the following provisions in the agreement:

Total franchise cost. How much money does it really take to own and operate the franchise? Not just for the franchise fee, but for everything. It's surprising how many people fail to take into consideration all the charges that may be assessed. Among these are—

- *Franchise fee*, granting you the right to engage in business as a franchised operation.
- *Physical facilities fees*, covering the costs of establishing you in an appropriate location (marketing research, construction, lease, and so on).
- *Equipment and fixtures costs*, covering the costs of outfitting your building.
- *Inventory and supplies costs*, covering the costs of stocking your business with the necessary inventory and supplies.
- *Royalty payments*, representing a percentage of annual gross sales (one of the requirements for operating the franchise).

- *Promotion costs,* covering your share of the advertising costs. (These may be included in the royalty payments.)
- *Finance charges,* including all interest due on loans made to the franchisee.

Only when you have added up all these charges (and any others that may be levied) can you determine the total franchise cost.

Contract life. What is the life of the contract? Does your right to operate the franchise extend indefinitely, or is it limited to a specific number of years? What are the renewal provisions? The average contract life, excluding renewal provisions, is fifteen years.

Termination clause. Often referred to as the franchisor's exit clause, the termination clause should be gone over with great care. Essentially, what it represents is the franchisor's right to terminate your relationship by canceling your contract or failing to renew it. This right is retained by the franchisor on the grounds that it is the only way to maintain standards and protect the company's image. Unfortunately, it can also be used to punish franchisees who allegedly fall out of line, even though there may be no good cause for doing so.

For your protection, make note of these four points:

1. What actions on your part constitute grounds for termination by the franchisor.
2. The method that will be used to determine the value of the franchise in the event of termination (original cost or fair market value).
3. Whether you have the right to terminate the agreement yourself and at what cost.
4. Whether you have the right, upon termination, to enter into direct competition with the franchisor in the franchise area.

Transfer of ownership. Do you have the right to sell or otherwise transfer ownership of the franchise to another party? In the majority of agreements, the franchisor reserves the right to buy back the franchise when the contract is terminated—often at the original price. Thus after investing several years' worth of time and money into your franchise, you could end up getting back only what you paid for it.

Franchise territory. The franchise territory is the selling area in which you are licensed to operate your franchise. In evaluating a prospective territory, you should determine the following:

1. Its sales potential (given local consumer demand and competition).
2. The characteristics (demographics and psychographics) of the neighborhood.
3. The territory's projected market growth.
4. Whether the franchisor is licensing others in the same territory.
5. Your right to open additional franchises in your territory or in other territories. Under existing antitrust laws, the franchisor has almost no legal power to stop you from branching out into other areas. However, bucking the franchise system is sure to strain your relationship.

Procedures. The procedures by which your franchise is expected to operate are included in the franchise agreement and/or the company's procedures manual. These can cover anything from the way to greet a customer to the way to keep the books. To safeguard your sanity later, take the time to familiarize yourself with them before you purchase the franchise. Remember that your way of doing business has to be compatible with the franchisor's way of doing business; otherwise, you're in for trouble.

Management training and assistance. What kind of management training and support can you count on the franchisor to provide? Some training programs are quite extensive, including one or more weeks at the franchisor's training headquarters, on-the-job training in an established franchise outlet, and continuing guidance once you're set up in your own franchise. Other training programs consist of little more than a few stapled-together pages of information, bolstered by an imaginary support system. Make sure the full details of the franchisor's training and assistance programs are spelled out in advance . . . and included in your contract. And don't forget to find out who foots the bill for the costs.

Promotional activities. What activities is the franchisor engaging in to promote the company's name and develop goodwill? Is advertising primarily at the local and regional level, or does it extend nationwide and beyond? Since one of the major selling points of a franchise is that it has a recognizable name, backed up by solid promotion, you need to know in advance the nature and extent of the company's promotional activities. And, once again, the matter of who pays for them comes up. Is your contribution included in the royalty fee, or is it an additional percentage of gross sales on top of that?

The franchise agreement merely sets down on paper the terms and conditions of the franchise relationship. As such, it isn't to be regarded with awe, but is to be explored as fully as possible. Don't let a lot of pages or legal jargon keep you from gaining a complete understanding of the agreement's contents. The best way to avoid getting burned is to enter into the relationship with your eyes open.

How to Find Franchise Opportunities

There are numerous sources of information you can refer to for help in finding franchise opportunities. The major sources are:

Newspapers. Chances are that you've already seen a variety of franchise offerings listed in the financial or classified section of your local newspaper.

Franchisors. If you already have a particular industry in mind, write directly to the franchisors in that field for details about the requirements for obtaining a franchise. By writing to more than one company, you can compare opportunities.

Trade publications. Read the trade publications for the industries that appeal to you. Franchisors seeking to expand their businesses will normally advertise in these.

Franchise associations. Franchise associations publish magazines and reports on franchising and sponsor exhibitions where you can meet with franchisor representatives.

Franchise specialists. For a fee, specialists in the area of franchising will help you find and research franchise opportunities. Their services include obtaining financial and marketing data on the companies being considered and providing recommendations.

Your banker. Your banker is tuned into the business community and probably can provide you with information on current franchise offerings or the names of people to contact.

The government. Government sources ranging from the Postal Service to the Federal Trade Commission can provide you with information on franchising. Probably the best one to start with is the Small Business Administration.

Franchising Checklist

Evaluating a franchise requires a clear head. Keeping track of all the information, weighing the pros and cons, and listening to your own feelings isn't easy. The Franchising Checklist on p. 174 should help you bring order out of the chaos.

FRANCHISING CHECKLIST

	Answer **yes or no**
1. Has the franchisor been in business long enough to have established a good reputation?	_____
2. Have you checked the Better Business Bureau, the Chamber of Commerce, Dun & Bradstreet, or your banker to find out about the franchisor's business reputation and credit rating?	_____
3. Has the franchisor shown you certified figures on the net profits of one or more going operations? Have you checked them yourself?	_____
4. Has the franchisor given you a specimen contract to study with the advice of counsel?	_____
5. Has the product or service been on the market long enough to gain good consumer acceptance?	_____
6. Would you buy the product or service on its merits?	_____
7. Is the product or service protected by a patent?	_____
8. Does product liability insurance protect both you and the franchisor?	_____
9. Does the contract give you an exclusive territory for the life of the franchise?	_____
10. Does the territory provide adequate sales potential?	_____
11. Have you made any study to determine whether the product or service you propose to sell has a market in your territory at the price you will have to charge?	_____
12. Will you be compelled to sell any new products or services introduced by the franchisor after you have opened the business?	_____
13. If there is an annual sales quota, can you retain your franchise if it is not met?	_____
14. Does the franchise fee seem reasonable?	_____
15. Do continuing royalties or payments of percentages of gross sales appear reasonable?	_____

Franchising Checklist (cont'd.)

	Answer yes or no
16. Does the cash investment include payment for fixtures and equipment?	————
17. Can you purchase supplies from another source when available at a lower price?	————
18. If you will be required to participate in company promotion and publicity by contributing to an advertising fund, will you have the right to veto any increase to the fund?	————
19. Will your training include an opportunity to observe and work with a successful franchise for a time?	————
20. Does the franchisor provide continuing assistance through supervisors who visit regularly?	————
21. Is the franchise agreement renewable?	————
22. Can you terminate the agreement if for some reason you are not happy about it?	————
23. May you sell the business to anyone you please?	————
24. Does your attorney approve of the contract?	————

Fourteen

Getting Help

The major cause of most business failures is management that lacks the knowledge, skills, experience, or simply the time needed to run a business efficiently. Since new businesses can rarely afford to hire the specialists who enable big business to carry out its objectives, they are at a distinct disadvantage. However, the way to compensate for this, and still keep payroll expenses to a minimum, is to utilize outside services.

There are many outside services that are willing and eager to help your business succeed. Whether you need help in obtaining financing, keeping your books in order, coming up with new concepts for products and ways to promote your business, training and motivating personnel, or solving a variety of business problems, there are services available. Some of these services cost money, but, surprisingly, many of them are provided free of charge.

Sources of Outside Help

Here are some of the individuals and institutions that can assist you in operating your business, listed in alphabetical order: accountants; advertising agencies; attorneys; bankers; chambers of commerce; colleges and universities; government agencies, including the Department of Commerce, economic development offices, Federal Trade Commission, Government Printing Office, Internal Revenue Service, Postal Service, and Small Business Administration; insurance agents; libraries; management and marketing consultants; temporary help services; and trade associations. Each source can provide you with specific and useful information that otherwise might not be readily accessible to your business.

Accountants

An accountant can be instrumental in helping you to keep your business operating on a sound financial basis. Even if you are already familiar with recordkeeping procedures, or employ a bookkeeper to maintain your records, the services of an outside accountant may still be required. In addition to designing an accounting system that's suitable for your specific needs, an accountant can also assist in the following areas:

- Determining cash requirements.
- Budgeting.
- Forecasting.
- Controlling costs.
- Preparing financial statements.
- Interpreting financial data.
- Obtaining loans.
- Preparing tax returns.

How to locate. You can find public accountants listed in the yellow pages of the telephone directory, but for best results it's advisable to try to locate one through a personal recommendation. Ask your banker or attorney to suggest an accountant. Since their work causes them to communicate with accountants regularly, both should be able to provide the names of accountants who can meet your requirements. Another approach is to contact one of the national or state accounting associations. Two of the larger associations are:

American Institute of Certified Public Accountants
666 Fifth Avenue, New York N.Y. 10019

National Society of Public Accountants
919 Eighteenth Street, N.W., Washington, D.C. 20006

Advertising Agencies

An advertising agency can help you to plan, produce, and place your business's advertising. Advertising agencies perform the following activities:

- Develop promotional strategies.
- Create advertising pieces (writing copy, designing graphics and layout, producing the finished product).
- Choose the appropriate media.
- Make sure that ads are run according to schedule.

Whether you need to use an advertising agency depends on the amount of advertising you intend to do.

How to locate. To find out which advertising agencies offer which services and how to contact them, check the *Standard Directory of Advertising Agencies,* available at many public libraries. Another source of agency information is to talk to media sales representatives and get their opinions about the various advertising agencies. The advertising agencies in your area should also be listed in the yellow pages.

Attorneys

An attorney can be useful to your business from the very start, helping you to determine which legal form of business is right for you, drawing up agreements, filing government paperwork, negotiating the lease or purchase of your building. Later on your attorney can continue to help by—

- Representing you in court.
- Providing legal advice.
- Interpreting legal documents.
- Assisting in tax planning.
- Helping you to comply with employment laws.
- Working out arrangements with creditors.
- Reorganizing the business, if needed.

How to locate. Your accountant or banker should be able to recommend an attorney. If not, your state's bar association can provide you with the names of attorneys in your area. Other sources of information include business acquaintances, friends, and the yellow pages.

Bankers

Your banker can be a valuable ally to your business, if you take the time to establish good rapport—preferably before you ask for a loan. The advice or information your banker can provide includes:

- How to open a checking account.
- How to obtain a line of credit.
- How to apply for a loan.
- How to prepare financial reports.
- How to bill customers.
- How to set up your payroll.

Furthermore, since bankers are constantly interacting with various segments of the community, your banker is likely to hear news that affects your business before you do.

Chambers of Commerce

Chambers of commerce are traditionally the information agencies of a community. Each chamber's goal is to represent and promote its area's economy, to encourage business and industrial investment, and to provide employment. As a new business owner, you should get in touch with your local chamber to find out what it has to offer (moral support, research data, general information about the community, or whatever). You might also decide to become a member. Chambers of commerce offer these benefits:

- They promote local businesses.
- They protect business interests.
- They act as the political voice of the business community.
- They are businesses united together.

Colleges and Universities

The colleges and universities in your area are a vast resource of information, skills, and training. They offer access to—

- The school's library for books, periodicals, government reports, reference works, maps, charts, audiovisual aids.
- Professional consultants in a variety of business-related areas.
- Labor in the form of students who are receiving training in your field.
- Additional education in the form of classes in management theory, business operations, advertising, and so on.
- Seminars especially for small business owners (often tied to the Small Business Administration).

Government Agencies

Agencies of government at the local, state, and federal levels can provide you with an abundance of useful information at little or no cost.

Department of Commerce. One government agency that specializes in business's concerns, the Department of Commerce oversees the research and distribution of information of direct interest to the economic community. These data are collected and made available to the public in the form of publications and reports, including—

- *Survey of Current Business*, a monthly periodical that provides updates on changes in the nation's economy and the levels of business production and distribution.
- *Census Bureau Reports*, covering such areas as population statistics (age, income, level of education, family status, and other demographic data) and manufacturing, business, and agricultural trends.

In addition to these reports, Commerce Department specialists can advise you in such specific areas as domestic and foreign marketing opportunities, contacting foreign representatives, and deciphering tariff and trade regulations.

How to locate. Department of Commerce publications are available at many public libraries or at the various department offices located throughout the United States. To find out the office that's closest to you, check your local phone directory white pages under "United States Government" or write to the Department of Commerce in Washington, D.C.

Economic development offices. Many communities maintain their own economic development offices. These differ from chambers of commerce in that they are maintained by local governments rather than local businesses. They can provide you with current statistical information regarding the economy, building activity, housing units, sales trends, population demographics, zoning, transportation, utilities, labor force, wages and salaries, community services, banks and savings and loan associations, traffic flows, and important telephone numbers.

Federal Trade Commission. The Federal Trade Commission regulates trade practices to protect the public against unfair methods of competition. It is empowered to collect information pertaining to business conduct and activities and distribute this to both government and the public. The information that is available includes guidelines on what constitutes deceptive pricing, deceptive guarantees, bait advertising, and other illegal practices.

To obtain the Federal Trade Commission's industry guides, write to: The Public Reference Section, Federal Trade Commission, Washington, D.C. 20580. These are free of charge.

Government Printing Office. The Government Printing Office oversees the publication and distribution of government documents, pamphlets, reports, and books on a variety of subjects, many of which are directly related to business. These are for sale, usually at nominal prices, at local Government Printing Office bookstores, which are generally located in federal buildings. If one isn't near you, or it doesn't stock a publication you want, write directly to the U.S. Government Printing Office, Superintendent of Documents, Washington, D.C. 20402. You will be sent a catalog of the publications available and any publications that you request.

Internal Revenue Service. The Internal Revenue Service can answer any questions you have concerning your federal income taxes. Tax specialists in local IRS offices can handle specific questions, or you can refer to any of the numerous IRS guides and publications, One particularly valuable guide is the *Tax Guide for Small Businesses,* which is updated annually. It contains approximately 200 pages of information covering such subjects as books and records, accounting periods, determining gross profit, deductible expenses, depreciation, tax credits, and ways to report income. This is available free of charge at your local IRS office. Some of the other IRS publications are listed at the end of this chapter.

Postal Service. The Postal Service can provide you with information that can help you reduce your mailing costs and use the mails more efficiently. The following publications can be obtained free from your local postmaster, or write to the U.S. Postal Service, Washington, D.C. 20260:

"Domestic Postage Rates and Fees"
"How to Address Mail"
"How to Pack and Wrap Parcels for Mailing"

"How to Prepare Second- and Third-Class Mailings"
"Mailing Permits"

The Postal Service also has available for sale a "Directory of Post Offices" and a "National ZIP Code Directory."

Small Business Administration. The Small Business Administration is designed to aid small businesses in the following ways:

- Helping to obtain financing.
- Providing management and technical assistance.
- Conducting business seminars and workshops.
- Assisting in procuring government contracts.

This is achieved through the operation of the 96 district offices, the distribution of publications, and the activities of the Service Corps of Retired Executives (SCORE) and the Active Corps of Executives (ACE), volunteer groups of professionals who assist the SBA in advising small businesses.

Financing by the SBA takes the form of direct and indirect loans to businesses. Loan proceeds can be used for working capital, for purchase of inventory, equipment, and supplies, or for building construction or expansion. The SBA also makes loans to help small businesses comply with federal air and water pollution regulations and meet occupational health and safety standards. In addition, economic opportunity loans are available to help persons who are socially or economically disadvantaged. Although money for venture or high-risk investments is difficult to obtain from the SBA, it licenses Small Business Investment Companies (SBICs), which *do* make such loans. For more information about SBA or SBIC lending practices, check Chapter Seven.

The SBA offers *management and technical assistance* in many forms. There are over 300 titles to choose from in its list of business publications. SBA form 115A lists free publications; SBA form 115B lists those that are for sale. A sampling of the titles is shown at the end of this chapter.

In-depth counseling is also provided by SBA management assistance staff, augmented by SCORE and ACE volunteers. Among the subject areas in which you can receive guidance are opening a business, marketing, advertising, profit goals, borrowing, accounting, bookkeeping, personnel, inventory controls, customer analysis, forecasting, and insurance. Meetings with these business counselors can be arranged through your local SBA field office. There is no charge for their services.

In order to help small entrepreneurs protect their investments, the SBA offers a variety of *seminars and workshops.* One that is of particular interest to prospective business owners is the Pre-Business Workshop. This is a free one-day session in which participants are helped to determine their readiness to go into business and advised of the steps involved in getting started. Once the decision is made to go ahead, the SBA assists participants in developing workable business plans. Other topics covered in workshops or seminars include:

- Sales Promotion and Advertising.
- Basic Business Operations.
- Business Planning.
- Women in Business.
- Foreign Trade.
- Retail Store Security.

The SBA's procurement assistance officers can guide you in the process of selling to the government and obtaining *government contracts.* Many of these details are also included in "Selling to the U.S Government," SBA publication PA-1, and "SBA's Procurement and Technical Assistance Programs," PA-3.

To find out which SBA district office is nearest to you, check the list at the end of this chapter.

Insurance Agents

An insurance agent can analyze your business's specific needs and help you to obtain adequate coverage. Aspects of risk management, that you should discuss with your agent include how to protect your assets, workers, and earnings and how to stay in compliance with the law. Since the welfare of your business is dependent on the safeguards you provide, finding a good insurance agent should be given a high priority.

How to locate. The best ways to find an insurance agent are through personal recommendations (your accountant, attorney, or banker may be able to suggest someone) and comparison shopping. Talking to different agents not only lets you evaluate the levels of coverage and compare the costs of different insurance plans but gives you an idea of which agent is the most knowledgeable about your type of business. You can find the names of insurance agents and companies in the yellow pages.

Libraries

Much of the information you need in order to operate your business can be obtained free of charge from libraries. The answers to many of your everyday business questions can be found not only in the books but in the assortment of magazines, newspapers, reference works, government publications, maps, charts, and audio/visual aids that are available. Management and marketing approaches, technical explanations, statistical data, industry information, trends and economic forecasts are just some of the subject areas in which you can find information.

How to locate. In addition to public libraries, there are also libraries sponsored by colleges and universities, private industry, trade and professional associations, labor unions, and research centers. The most useful of these generally have separate business reference sections. To find the libraries in your area, check your local telephone directory.

Management and Marketing Consultants

Management and marketing consultants can detect weaknesses in your methods of operation or your marketing strategy and recommend corrective measures. They can also be of help *before* problems arise, providing advice on new product development, marketing research, business expansion, administration, employee motivation, cost control, security, and so on.

Many businesses make a practice of calling in a management or marketing consultant whenever a major decision in these areas needs to be made. This enables the business owner to benefit not only from the consultant's knowledge and experience, but from something equally valuable: the consultant's objectivity. Unlike employees, consultants have nothing to gain or lose from the outcome of a decision. Furthermore, the variety of their contacts in the business community usually gives them a broader perspective.

How to locate. The best way to locate a management or marketing consultant is through recommendations, preferably from the consultant's satisfied clients. Otherwise, you can check the listings in one of the several directories of consultants available at public libraries or in the yellow pages.

Temporary Help Services

There are currently more than a thousand temporary help service firms in the United States, providing experienced and well-qualified temporary help in a moment's notice. You may contract for a typist, switchboard operator, bookkeeper, machinist, truck driver, or other office, professional, and industrial workers. The temporary help service firm takes care of all screening, interviewing, and testing of applicants, as well as the checking of references.

How to locate. Temporary help service firms can be located through personal recommendations, local chambers of commerce, or the yellow pages.

Trade Associations

Trade associations are organizations whose members are in the same business or industry (garment industry, banking and finance, restaurants, automotive repair). The concerns and services of trade associations are directed at helping members to improve their operating efficiency and cope with business problems. This help is in the form of—

- *Accounting services.* Providing accounting forms and manuals, ratio data, cost studies, and consultations.
- *Advertising and marketing services.* Providing advertising materials and forecasts of future demand levels and trends.
- *Publicity and public relations activities.* Providing members and the mass media with information about industry activities.
- *Educational programs.* Providing a variety of training courses and aids to assist business owners and employees in developing their skills.
- *Research activities.* Providing members and government with statistics about the industry—method of operation, product standards, certifying and grading, and so on.
- *Employee relations programs.* Providing members with information about industry wages, work schedules, and fringe benefits as well as assisting in the negotiation of labor contracts.
- *Government relations programs.* Providing members with a collective voice to use in communicating with the government and informing members of government actions pertaining to their businesses.

In addition, trade associations are active in public service, consumerism, and environmental safety. Of course, not all associations provide all these services. To find out which ones are provided, contact the association in your field of business.

How to locate. To obtain information on trade associations or find out which ones represent your industry, write to:

American Society of Association Executives
1101 Sixteenth Street N.W., Washington, D.C. 20036

Publications available at most public libraries:

- *National Trade and Professional Associations of the United States and Canada*, Columbia Books, Inc., Publishers, Washington, D.C.
- *Encyclopedia of Associations, Vol. 1, National Organizations of the U.S.*, Gale Research Co., Detroit, Michigan.

The following is a sampling of government publications, as well as a list of SBA Field Offices.

INTERNAL REVENUE SERVICE TAX PUBLICATIONS

TITLE	No.
Employer's Tax Guide, Circular E	15
Your Federal Income Tax	17
Federal Social Security Tax Guide for Employers in the Virgin Islands, Guam and American Samoa	80
Farmer's Tax Guide	225
Federal Fuel Tax Credit or Refund for Nonhighway and Transit Users	378
Self-Employment Tax Tables	421
Entertainment, Travel, and Gift Expenses	463
Estimated Tax and Tax Withholding	505
Your Federal Income Tax Calendar	509
Excise Taxes	510
Self-Employment Tax	533

Internal Revenue Service Tax Publications (Cont'd)

INTERNAL REVENUE SERVICE TAX PUBLICATIONS (CONT'D)

Tax Information on Unemployment Compensation	905
Targeted Jobs and WIN Credits	906
Filing Requirements for Employee Benefit Plans	1048

SMALL BUSINESS ADMINISTRATION PUBLICATIONS
SAMPLING OF TITLES FROM FORM SBA 115A
FREE PUBLICATIONS—MANAGEMENT AIDS

TITLE	No.
The ABCs of Borrowing	170
Effective Industrial Advertising for Small Plants	178
Breaking the Barriers to Small Business Planning	179
Checklist for Developing a Training Program	186
Using Census Data in Small Plant Marketing	187
Developing a List of Prospects	188
Should You Make or Buy Components?	189
Measuring Sales Force Performance	190
Delegating Work and Responsibility	191
Profile Your Customers to Expand Industrial Sales	192
What Is the Best Selling Price?	193
Marketing Planning Guidelines	194
Setting Pay for Your Management Jobs	195
Expand Oversees Sales With Commerce Department Help	199
Pointers on Negotiating DOD Contracts	204
Keep Pointed Toward Profit	206
Pointers on Scheduling Production	207
Problems in Managing a Family-Owned Business	208
The Equipment Replacement Decision	212
Finding a New Product for Your Company	216
Business Plan for Small Manufacturers	218
Solid Waste Management in Industry	219
Basic Budgets for Profit Planning	220

SAMPLING OF TITLES FROM SBA 115A (CONT'D)

FREE PUBLICATIONS—SMALL MARKETERS' AIDS

Free Publications—Small Marketers' Aids (Cont'd)

Small Business Administration Publications
Sampling of titles from form SBA 115B
For-Sale Booklets–Small Business Management Series

Sampling of SBA 115B booklets (Cont'd)

SBA Field Office Addresses

Boston	Massachusetts 02114, 150 Causeway Street
Holyoke	Massachusetts 01040, 302 High Street
Augusta	Maine 04330, 40 Western Avenue, Room 512
Concord	New Hampshire 03301, 55 Pleasant Street
Hartford	Connecticut 06103, One Financial Plaza
Montpelier	Vermont 05602, 87 State Street, P.O. Box 605
Providence	Rhode Island 02903, 57 Eddy Street
New York	New York 10007, 26 Federal Plaza, Room 3214
Albany	New York 12207, Twin Towers Building, Room 922
Elmira	New York 14904, 180 State Street, Room 412
Hato Rey	Puerto Rico 00918, Federal Office Building, Carlos Chardon Avenue
Newark	New Jersey 07102, 970 Broad Street, Room 1635
Camden	New Jersey 08104, East Davis Street
Syracuse	New York 13202, 100 South Clinton Street, Room 1073
Buffalo	New York 14202, 111 West Huron Street
St. Thomas	Virgin Islands 00801, Franklin Building
Philadelphia	Bala Cynwyd, Pennsylvania 19004, One Bala Cynwyd Plaza
Harrisburg	Pennsylvania 17108, 1500 North Second Street
Wilkes-Barre	Pennsylvania 18702, 20 North Pennsylvania Avenue
Baltimore	Towson, Maryland 21204, 7800 York Road
Wilmington	Delaware 19801, 844 King Street
Clarksburg	West Virginia 26301, 109 N. 3rd Street
Charleston	West Virginia 25301, Charleston National Plaza, Suite 628
Pittsburgh	Pennsylvania 15222, 1000 Liberty Avenue
Richmond	Virginia 23240, 400 N. 8th Street, Room 3015
Washington	D.C. 20417, 1030 15th Street, NW., Suite 250
Atlanta	Georgia 30309, 1720 Peachtree Road, NW., Suite 600
Biloxi	Mississippi 39530, 111 Fred Haise Boulevard
Birmingham	Alabama 35205, 908 South 20th Street
Charlotte	North Carolina 28202, 230 South Tryon Street, Suite 700
Greenville	North Carolina 27834, 215 South Evans Street
Columbia	South Carolina 29201, 1801 Assembly Street
Coral Gables	Florida 33134, 2222 Ponce de Leon Boulevard
Jackson	Mississippi 39201, 200 East Pascagoula Street
Jacksonville	Florida 32202, 400 W. Bay Street
West Palm Beach	Florida 33402, 701 Clematis Street
Tampa	Florida 33607, 1802 North Trask Street, Suite 203
Louisville	Kentucky 40202, 600 Federal Place, Room 188
Nashville	Tennessee 37219, 404 James Robertson Parkway, Suite 1012
Knoxville	Tennessee 37902, 502 South Gay Street, Room 307
Memphis	Tennessee 38103, 167 North Main Street

SBA Field Office Addresses (Cont'd)

Chicago	Illinois 60604, 219 South Dearborn Street
Springfield	Illinois 62701, 1 North Old State Capitol Plaza
Cleveland	Ohio 44199, 1240 East 9th Street, Room 317
Columbus	Ohio 43215, 85 Marconi Boulevard
Cincinnati	Ohio 45202, 550 Main Street, Room 5524
Detroit	Michigan 48226, 477 Michigan Avenue
Marquette	Michigan 49885, 540 West Kaye Avenue
Indianapolis	Indiana 46204, 575 North Pennsylvania Street
Madison	Wisconsin 53703, 122 West Washington Avenue, Room 713
Milwaukee	Wisconsin 53233, 735 West Wisconsin Avenue
Eau Claire	Wisconsin 54701, 500 South Barstow Street, Room B9AA
Minneapolis	Minnesota 55402, 12 South Sixth Street
Dallas	Texas 75202, 1100 Commerce Street
Albuquerque	New Mexico 87110, 5000 Marble Avenue, NE.
Houston	Texas 77002, 1 Allen Center, Suite 705
Little Rock	Arkansas 72201, 611 Gaines Street, P.O. Box 1401
Lubbock	Texas 79401, 1205 Texas Avenue
El Paso	Texas 79902, 4100 Rio Bravo, Suite 300
Lower Rio Grande Valley	Harlingen, Texas 78550, 222 East Van Buren, Suite 500
Corpus Christi	Texas 78408, 3105 Leopard Street, P.O. Box 9253
Marshall	Texas 75670, 100 South Washington Street, Room G12
New Orleans	Louisiana 70113, 1001 Howard Avenue
Shreveport	Louisiana 71163, 500 Fannin Street
Oklahoma City	Oklahoma 73102, 200 NW. 5th Street
San Antonio	Texas 78206, 727 East Durango, Room A-513
Kansas City	Missouri 64106, 1150 Grand Avenue
Des Moines	Iowa 50309, 210 Walnut Street
Omaha	Nebraska 68102, Nineteenth and Farnam Streets
St. Louis	Missouri 63101, Mercantile Tower, Suite 2500
Wichita	Kansas 67202, 110 East Waterman Street
Denver	Colorado 80202, 721 19th Street, Room 407
Casper	Wyoming 82601, 100 East B Street, Room 4001
Fargo	North Dakota 58102, 653 2nd Avenue, North, Room 218
Helena	Montana 59601, 613 Helena Avenue, P.O. Box 1690
Salt Lake City	Utah 84138, 125 South State Street, Room 2237
Rapid City	South Dakota 57701, 515 9th Street
Sioux Falls	South Dakota 57102, 8th and Main Avenue
San Francisco	California 94105, 211 Main Street
Fresno	California 93721, 1229 N Street
Sacramento	California 95825, 2800 Cottage Way
Honolulu	Hawaii 96813, 1149 Bethel Street, Room 402
Agana	Guam 96910, Ada Plaza Center Building, P.O. Box 927
Los Angeles	California 90071, 350 South Figueroa Street
Las Vegas	Nevada 89101, 301 East Stewart
Reno	Nevada 89504, 300 Booth Street
Phoenix	Arizona 85004, 112 North Central Avenue
San Diego	California 92188, 880 Front Street
Seattle	Washington 98174, 915 Second Avenue
Anchorage	Alaska 99501, 1016 West Sixth Avenue, Suite 200
Fairbanks	Alaska 99701, 501½ Second Avenue
Boise	Idaho 83701, 216 North 8th Street, P.O. Box 2618
Portland	Oregon 97204, 1220 South West Third Avenue
Spokane	Washington 99120, Courthouse Bldg., Room 651, P.O. Box 2167

Suggested Reading

Brownstone, David M. *Successful Selling Skills for Small Business* (New York: Wiley, 1978).

Chruden, Herbert J., and Arthur W. Sherman. *Personnel Management* (Cincinnati: Southwester, 1976).

Cooper, Alfred M. *How to Supervide People* (New York: McGraw-Hill, 1973).

Curtis, Robert. *Security Control: Internal Theft* (New York: Chain Store Publishing, 1973).

Dible, Donald M. *Up Your Own Organization* (Santa Clara, Calif.: Entrepreneur Press, 1971).

Doyle, Dennis M. *Efficient Accounting and Record-Keeping* (New York: Wiley, 1977).

Dyer, Mary L. *Practical Bookkeeping for the Small Business* (Chicago: Regnery, 1976).

Goldstein, Arnold S. *Strategies and Techniques for Saving the Financially Distressed Small Business* (New York: Pilot Books, 1976).

James, Don L. *Retailing Today* (New York: Harcourt, 1975).

Keeling, B. Lewis. *Payroll Records and Accounting* (Cincinnati: Southwestern, 1976).

Lev, Baruch, *Financial Statement Analysis: A New Approach (Englewood Cliffs, N.J.: Prentice-Hall, 1974).*

Loffel, Egon W. Financing Your Business (New York: Wiley, 1977).
_____ *Protecting Your Business* (New York: Wiley, 1977).

Malickson, David L., and John W. Nason. *Advertising—How to Write the Kind That Works* (New York: Scribner, 1977).

Mangold, Maxwell. *How to Buy a Small Business* (New York: Pilot Books, 1976).

Margolis, Neal. and N. Paul Harmon. *Accounting Essentials* (New York: Wiley, 1972).

Moscarello, Louis C. *Retail Accounting and Financial Control* (New York: Ronald Press, 1976).

Powers, Melvin. *How to Get Rich in Mail Order* (North Hollywood, Calif.: Wilshire Book, 1980).

Richards, Gerald F., *Tax Planning Opportunities* (New York: Wiley, 1977).

Richman, Eugene. *Practical Guide to Managing People* (Englewood Cliffs, N.J.: Prentice-Hall, 1975).

Seder, John W. *Credit and Collections* (New York: Wiley, 1977).

Siegel, Gonnie McClung, *How to Advertise and Promote Your Small Business* (New York: Wiley, 1978).

Smith, Cynthia S. *How to Get Big Results from a Small Advertising Budget* (New York: Hawthorn, 1973).

Vaughn, Charles L. *Franchising* (Lexington, Mass: Heath, 1974).

Index